Twayne's United States Authors Series

Sylvia E. Bowman, *Editor*

INDIANA UNIVERSITY

Mary Ellen Chase

ABOUT THE AUTHOR

PERRY D. WESTBROOK is Professor of English at the State University of New York, Albany. He was a Phi Beta Kappa scholar at Columbia College and received his M.A. and Ph.D. degrees from Columbia University, commuting between Albany and New York City for the latter. His dissertation on rural New England writers was published to scholarly acclaim.

Professor Westbrook has contributed often to such journals as *Notes & Queries, College English,* and *The New England Quarterly,* and he is the author of five published mystery novels. While on a Guggenheim Fellowship in 1953-54 he wrote a study of a fishing village near Mary Ellen Chase's home town of Blue Hill, Maine, published as *Biography of an Island.* His other books include *The Greatness of Man; an Essay on Dostoyevsky and Whitman,* as well as a book on horsemanship written in collaboration with one of his three daughters.

He lives with his family on a farm near Albany.

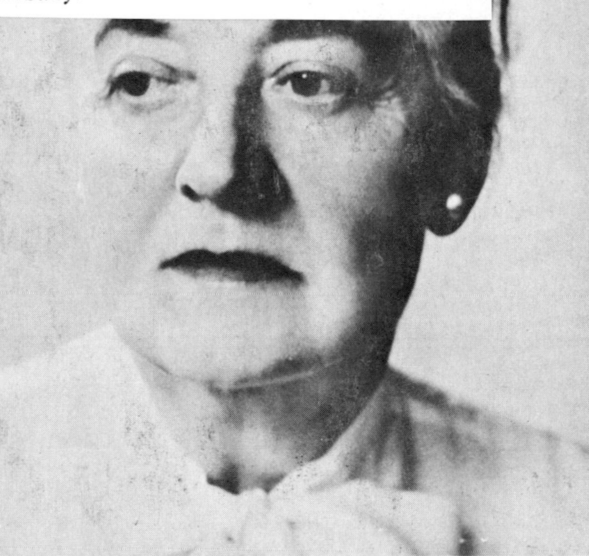

Photo by RAMSEY & MUSPRATT

MARY ELLEN CHASE

MARY ELLEN CHASE

by PERRY D. WESTBROOK
State University of New York

 86

Twayne Publishers, Inc. :: New York

Library of Congress Catalog Card Number: 65-18905

MANUFACTURED IN THE UNITED STATES OF AMERICA BY
UNITED PRINTING SERVICES, INC.
NEW HAVEN, CONN.

For
Arlen

Preface

MARY ELLEN CHASE held her first class in 1906 in a one-room school on the Maine coast. She sold her first story—to *The American Boy*—in 1909. In the half century and more following these dates she not only became one of America's most distinguished professors of literature and a beloved and sought-after lecturer but has also published thirty-five books—fiction, essays, Biblical studies, biography, autobiography—many short stories, and hundreds of magazine articles and reviews. Most of her books are still in print, some of them thirty years or more after original publication, and many have been translated not only into the major languages of Europe but also into those of India and the Far East. An unfavorable review of a Mary Ellen Chase book is difficult to find. She has won the respect of both readers and critics to a degree few writers enjoy.

This sort of accomplishment demands attention. It is the purpose of the present book to review Miss Chase's many literary contributions to the national culture. My approach has been to examine her background and development through a study of her autobiographical books, themselves among her most impressive achievements. Next, after a brief account of her earliest fiction, I have proceeded to her novels about Maine; for these not only constitute her most admired work but are most closely related to her autobiographical writings. I then proceed to a consideration of those novels that treat characters and settings not exclusively of her native Maine coast. The last chapters deal with her work in biography, the informal essay, literary criticism, and juvenile fiction and with her remarkable series, now numbering four volumes and not yet terminated, on the Bible. Through all of this output I have attempted to trace the unifying thread of Miss Chase's cherished New England heritage—its values, its humor, its ideals.

I could not have completed this work without the aid of many persons. Miss Chase herself, in letters and in conversation, has set me right on details of her life and publications. Professor Richard Cary, Curator of Rare Books and Manuscripts at the

Library of Colby College, has helped inestimably in supplying information not already printed in his Mary Ellen Chase bibliography in the *Colby Library Quarterly* of March, 1962. To the Librarians of the University of Maine; of the United States Information Library at Madras, India; of the New York State Library; and, above all, of the Library of the State University of New York at Albany, I am grateful for prompt, efficient, and cheerful responses to my demands upon their time and skill. To my wife, Arlen Westbrook, I am indebted for a painstakingly critical reading of the manuscript and for much of the labor of preparing it for the printers.

PERRY D. WESTBROOK

State University of New York, Albany
October, 1964

Acknowledgments

The author wishes to express his gratitude to the following for permission to quote from copyrighted material:

To Mary Ellen Chase for general permission to quote from those of her works on which she holds copyright.

To the Macmillan Company for quotations from *Mary Peters*, *Silas Crockett*, *This England*, *Dawn in Lyonesse*, *A Goodly Fellowship*, *Windswept*, *The Bible and the Common Reader*, *Jonathan Fisher, Maine Parson, 1768-1847*, *The Plum Tree*, and *Abby Aldrich Rockefeller*.

To W. W. Norton and Company for quotations from *The White Gate*, *Life and Language in the Old Testament*, *The Edge of Darkness*, *The Lovely Ambition*, and *The Psalms for the Common Reader*.

To Holt, Rinehart, and Winston, Inc., for quotations from *The Golden Asse and Other Essays*, *Constructive Theme Writing for College Freshmen*, *The Silver Shell*, and *A Goodly Heritage*.

Contents

Chronology

1887	Mary Ellen Chase born February 24 in Blue Hill, Maine, the second in a family of eight children. Descendant of sea-captains, teachers and preachers; daughter of a country lawyer.
1892	Entered same school attended by her father and grandfather.
1900	Entered Blue Hill Academy.
1904	Entered University of Maine at Orono.
1906-1907	Interrupted her college course to teach in one-room schools in Buck's Harbor and in West Brooksville, Maine.
1909	Took her A.B. degree at University of Maine; published her first story, a contribution to *The American Boy,* entitled "His Place on the Eleven"; began teaching at Hillside Home School in Spring Green, Wisconsin.
1912	Took teaching position at Miss Moffat's School for Girls in Chicago.
1913	Spent summer in Germany, in Berlin and the Harz Mountains, to study the language.
1914	Left Miss Moffat's School; father died; began her three-year recuperation from tuberculosis in Montana, resting, reading, writing, and teaching in high school.
1915	Publication of her first book, *His Birthday,* quickly followed by other books for children.
1917	Entered University of Minnesota Graduate School to work for doctorate.
1918	Received M.A. from University of Minnesota; took instructorship there in freshman English; published short story "A Return to Constancy" in *Harper's.*
1922	Passed oral examinations at the University of Minnesota and received doctorate; became assistant professor of English at University of Minnesota.
1923	Began teaching three hours a week at College of St. Catherine in St. Paul; shared in convent life, though not a Roman Catholic.

1926 Publication of *Mary Christmas;* beginning of thirty years of teaching at Smith College, Northampton, Massachusetts.

1927 Publication of her doctor's dissertation, *Thomas Hardy from Serial to Novel;* and of *Uplands.*

1928 Honorary degree of Doctor of Letters at University of Maine.

1931 $2,500 prize awarded to her by *Pictorial Review* for the story "Salesmanship."

1932 Publication of *A Goodly Heritage.*

1933 Honorary Doctor of Letters at Bowdoin.

1934 Publication of *Mary Peters.*

1934-1936 Residence in Cambridgeshire, England; writing of *Silas Crockett* (published 1935) and *This England* (1936).

1937 Honorary Doctor of the Humanities from Colby College.

1938 Publication of *Dawn in Lyonesse.*

1939 *A Goodly Fellowship.*

1941 *Windswept.*

1944 *The Bible and the Common Reader.*

1947 Studied Hebrew at Cambridge, England.

1948 Publication of *Jonathan Fisher, Maine Parson, 1768-1847;* invited to help with Revised Standard Version of the Bible "to make the English fall better." Doctor of Letters from Northeastern College.

1949 Doctor of Letters from Smith College.

1954 *The White Gate.*

1955 Publication of *Life and Language in the Old Testament;* retirement from active teaching at Smith but continued residence at Northampton with part of each winter in England.

1957 *The Edge of Darkness.*

1960 *The Lovely Ambition.*

1961 *The Psalms for the Common Reader* and *The Fishing Fleets of New England.*

1963 *The Prophets for the Common Reader.*

Mary Ellen Chase

CHAPTER *1*

'The Lines Are Fallen to Me in Pleasant Places'

DOSTOYEVSKY once wrote: "You must know that there is nothing higher and stronger and more wholesome and good for life than some good memory, especially a memory of childhood." Mary Ellen Chase chose this passage as a motto for her novel *Mary Peters*. The passage continues: "If a man carries many such memories with him into life, he is safe to the end of his days, and if one has only one good memory left in one's heart, even that may some time be the means of saving us." Miss Chase's own childhood provided such memories in great quantity, and she interprets her later life, as teacher or author, in terms of them. She herself knows better than any one else how fortunate she has been in the place and time of her upbringing, in her education, and in the family into which she was born. Quite naturally, then, three of her most important works—*A Goodly Heritage*, *A Goodly Fellowship*, and *The White Gate*—are devoted to recapturing her Maine girlhood and to recording her experiences as a beginning teacher and as a student in graduate school. These volumes are, of course, the best introduction to Miss Chase as a person and an artist.

I *A Village of Kindly Engendure*

Mary Ellen Chase was born on February 24, 1887, in the eastern Maine coastal town of Blue Hill, which she has described, in the words of Charles Lamb, as "a place of kindly engendure."[1] In *A Goodly Heritage* she traces her descent back to settlers from Massachusetts who founded Blue Hill in the 1760's. In her mother's family was a tradition of preaching and school-teaching. The mother herself was an impassioned lover of literature and for a time taught Latin at Blue Hill Academy. On her father's side, Miss Chase's ancestors were seafarers of that far-traveled breed who, in Sarah Orne Jewett's words, "did not mistake their native parishes for the whole of the world instead of a part thereof." Of the Maine maritime tradition, in which her fore-bears figure so importantly, Mary Ellen Chase is justly proud, and she has made it the subject of her best writing. Of the old shipmasters she has this to say: "While they sailed, they gave to their children and grandchildren the example as well as the knowledge of endurance and of courage, of resiliency after disaster, of the satisfaction of playing a game with Fortune, provided one were well fortified by nature and by training for such a gamble. When they left the sea . . . , they brought to their homes and to their communities a perspective and a power of evaluation which has left its mark on succeeding generations."[2] From her paternal grandmother, who had sailed long and far with her sea-captain husband, Mary Ellen Chase heard stories that took their place among her most germinal memories. Her father did not go to sea; instead, he became a lawyer. His enthusiasm for history and literature, added to his wife's love of books, made the Chase household a place where children learned to read as naturally as they learned to walk. In her reminiscence of early childhood, Miss Chase has as much to say of the books she lived with as of her friends and family.

One must know something about Blue Hill if one is to understand Mary Ellen Chase's feeling for it and her artistic debt to it. She describes the village in detail, of course, in her autobiographical books, particularly in *A Goodly Heritage,* as well as under faint disguise in much of her fiction. The town is located at the head of Blue Hill Bay between Penobscot Bay and Mt. Desert Island—the most mountainous stretch of coast on the Atlantic seaboard. Just back of the village rises Blue Hill itself, a low spruce-clad cone that dominates the bay and gives it its name. To the east are the somewhat higher and rockier Mt. Desert Hills; to the west, in the blue-gray distance, the Camden Hills. The bay which is eight or ten miles wide and as many long, is sprinkled with rocky islands and islets. It is separated from the ocean by a chain of rather large islands, the most important of which are the fishing communities of Swans Island and Frenchboro.

Blue Hill Bay has long been frequented by yachtsmen, among them Franklin D. Roosevelt, who in World War II chose it as the location for the famous meeting with Churchill which resulted in the Atlantic Charter. From the sixteenth century onward, this part of the coast around Mt. Desert was of interest to navigators and explorers. It was first mapped by Champlain; and, even before the settling of Plymouth, the French attempted to colonize it. Though quickly driven out by the English, the French left a few stray traders and trappers on the islands and in Castine, a village not far from Blue Hill. The early history of the coast has always been fascinating to the more recent inhabitants; Americans, and particularly New Englanders and Southerners, make the most of whatever sense of the past their home region affords them.

At the close of the American Revolution settlers in great numbers poured eastward from the overpopulated townships on Massachusetts Bay and joined the few pioneers, among whom were Miss Chase's forebears, who had arrived before the war. Sailing down the coast in their sturdy Chebacco boats, these newcomers soon established most of the island and mainland towns now existent east of the Penobscot. By stock, they were exclusively English, even Irish and Scotsmen being rare among them. To the present day, despite some admixture of French and Portuguese, these coastal communities are culturally homogeneous to a degree unusual in the United States.

The settlers brought with them the best of their New England civilization as embodied in church and school. Till the beginning of the twentieth century, the influence of religion in a town like Blue Hill was decisive. In her girlhood Mary Ellen Chase participated as a matter of course in the activities of the local Congregational Church. The lengthy sermons on theological subjects meant little to her when a child; more memorable was her father's weekly placing of a five-dollar bill in the plate, the only paper offering in the entire collection.

But the routine of weekly worship Sunday after Sunday grooved itself into her being, becoming as necessary as food or sleep to her life. As she approached adolescence, she began to fret about conversion—a "direct experience" of religion required of a candidate for membership in orthodox Calvinistic churches. Without conversion and the overwhelming spiritual change it was supposed to bring about, one could not be considered a true Christian, one of the Communion of Saints. Failure to experience conversion was, therefore, a stigma on the individual and his family. Achievement of it was cause for rejoicing and tearful congratulations that could be almost as embarrassing to the newly "regenerate" as his previous state of unregeneracy. To aid the young people in their struggle for grace, the first week of January was set aside every year for prayers and meetings designed to bring the soul to crisis. Painful introspection was the order of the day; among the high-school students anxiety grew as they prodded and questioned one another about their spiritual condition. At Blue Hill were fomented states of group hysteria reminiscent of those of Jonathan Edwards' heyday in Northampton. For the sensitive and overconscientious, this time could be a period of hell, as it apparently was for Miss Chase[3]; but she finally managed to convince herself and others that she was "saved."

This emphasis on religion had a permanent effect on Mary Ellen Chase. To the present day she has been actively religious and has respected the religious life, whether that of the Protestants, or of the Roman Catholics, among whose nuns she has made many close friendships. Not satisfied with the rigidities and starkness of old-time Congregationalism, she herself eventually became an Episcopalian. One of her major interests as a teacher at Smith College has been her course in the Bible as literature; and her books *The Bible and the Common Reader, The Psalms for the Common Reader, Life and Language in the Old Testament,* and *The Prophets for the Common Reader,* as well as a collection of Biblical readings that she edited, have enjoyed a wide readership.

Second only to the church as a bulwark of civilization in rural New England was education. The Maine academies, among which the one at Blue Hill has long been outstanding, were founded to provide sound high-school instruction to the children in the towns and from surrounding areas. These schools maintained rigorous standards; their faculties were college trained; and their curriculum, at least for those planning to go to college, was "classical." Mary Ellen Chase cannot say too much in praise of Blue Hill Academy, which she attended; the Latin, Greek, and English courses there were indispensable foundation stones for all her later studies. Her teachers, some of whom later became nationally famous as professors and scholars, were an inspiration to her during her own long teaching career. Learning was the chief business in such schools, and learning was respected in the community at large—especially among the solid families like Mary Ellen Chase's.

Henry Ward Beecher, himself brought up in a Connecticut town with religious and educational traditions not unlike those of Blue Hill, once said that the village was the brood comb of New England's intellectual life.[4] Too many persons have the notion that Boston and New Haven are New England's only cultural repositories. Nothing could be more mistaken. Most of the region's famous contributors to the intellectual and political life of the nation—Jonathan Edwards, Longfellow, T. B. Aldrich, Hawthorne, Emily Dickinson, Noah Webster, E. A. Robinson, Daniel Webster, Rufus Jones, Whittier, the Beechers, the Stowes, Edward Bellamy—were products of the villages or of the lesser ports.

The influence of village culture was not confined solely to the six northeastern states; it was spread wherever New Englanders migrated, across much of the northern half of the country, and, for that matter, on to Hawaii. Such communities ensured for their young people a unique and invaluable combination of a sound education in the humanities and sciences, a soil where religious roots could strike down deeply and permanently, and the innocence and sense of security that bless a childhood in a closely knit, prosperous society living by a traditional set of values. A deeply ingrained sense of right and wrong, a self-reliance fortified no doubt by study in school of Emerson's famous essay on the subject, a well-disciplined and well-stocked mind are enviable equipment for a person starting out in life. They are the aims, presumably, of all American education; they are supposed to flourish in American civilization as nowhere else; but it is doubtful if they were ever so successfully inculcated as in communities like Blue Hill during and before Mary Ellen Chase's childhood there.

The Maine coastal towns had distinctive characteristics and advantages not shared, perhaps, by the inland towns. The Yankee virtues of initiative, ingenuity, and versatility existed on the coast in concentration. Basic to the way of life was the combining of farming, fishing, and seafaring. Much fiction and non-fiction has been written about the Maine farmer-fisherman-shipmaster who would spend the spring and summer in his fields, the autumn on the Grand Banks, and the winter sailing a schooner in either the coastwise or the transoceanic trade. Such men would be equally skillful at planting potatoes, setting a halibut trawl, or riding out a West Indian hurricane. To them the idea of being able to do just one thing was unthinkable. They were adept at many trades, were at home in many environments, and were at ease with many points of view.

But on the Maine coast, until the present century, seafaring, more than farming or even fishing, was the most widely followed calling. Many shipowners in Blue Hill, as elsewhere, were deep-water skippers, familiar with all the seas; these men, often accompanied by their wives, would absent themselves for years on voyages that carried them around the world. But there was hardly a farmer or a farmer's son who had not spent some time at sea either on a family vessel or in the hire of some other owner. All these persons, whether sailing lumber schooners to Boston or New York or clippers to Hong Kong or Bombay, cherished a fierce attachment to the little New England port where they and their ancestors had been born. There they would retire in a stately cupolaed mansion on the hill or in a one-story cottage down by the cove, depending on how financially successful they had been in their wanderings about the world. Never were people so devoted to home and yet so frequently and for such long periods away from it. There was never any question as to where home was. Marriages with foreign women, indeed with other than New England women, were rare. Thus the citizens of towns like Blue Hill were distinguished by a cosmopolitanism allied with a ferocious localism; and, owing to the many-sided lives they lived, they developed a remarkable adaptability and self-confidence. They were pretty well convinced that they were God's chosen ones and that their villages were in the most desirable portion of His earth. Persons with such a background would, and did, venture forth into the world, whether as sailors, teachers, editors, or businessmen, with the assurance of a success that seldom in fact eluded them.

The very architecture of the New England village, either inland or on the coast, suggests at its best the high degree of stability and self-sufficiency of its inhabitants. There is no clash with the environment; the buildings fit into the landscape as naturally as the boulders in the surrounding fields and the pines in the forests. The houses are spacious, simple, clean in line and surface; the Greek-influenced churches bespeak a connection with a life-giving tradition. The trees, commons, lawns, and gardens bring the beauty and calm of nature to the very walls of the dwellings. Villages elsewhere in America possess these qualities, but they are not very numerous. Much more usual is a jarring clash of human habitation and the countryside.

During Mary Ellen Chase's lifetime, much has changed in the New England village—and much had changed before her birth. The days of the circumnavigating voyagers had passed not only in Blue Hill but throughout New England; but many of the old adventurous captains were still alive, dwelling in retirement in their square, elm-shaded mansions that lined the village streets. The farming-seafaring life still prevailed among the less well-to-do, but in general prosperity had declined seriously. The tiny, stony farms, the small fishing and coastwise cargo vessels could no longer compete successfully in the American economy where largeness, whether in farms or ships, was essential to making a profit. In Maine, poverty was on the increase; the rural slum, with all its shiftlessness, moral laxness, and at times degeneracy, was and is widespread.

Yet in some towns the change had been less calamitous than in others, and Blue Hill was among the more fortunate. It was benefiting from the establishment of regular communications which were slowly drawing the seaboard communities out of their isolation. The coastwise passenger steamers, which passed into history at the beginning of World War II, were making the ports along their routes easily accessible to one another, as well as to the larger cities—Bangor, Portland, Boston. Later came the railroad and then the automobile, and—with the exception of the islands, which were plunged back into isolation with the loss of the steamboats—even the remotest reaches of the coast were brought into continuous contact with the rest of the state and nation.

On the steamboats came summer cottagers, and they continued to come in increasing numbers by railroad and automobile. Quite understandably Blue Hill with its rocky shores and sweeping upland pastures and lovely architecture was exceptionally attractive to the "rusticators," who were less flatteringly known as the "summer complaint." The influx had begun in Mary Ellen Chase's childhood and was causing characteristic strains and tensions in the village life; Miss Chase deals with them in several of her novels with Maine settings.

II A Goodly Heritage

A sensitive and intelligent girl growing up in Blue Hill could not but feel and think with the psalmist: "The lines are fallen to me in pleasant places; yea, I have a goodly heritage." This is precisely how Mary Ellen Chase felt and thought, and it was from this same verse of the psalms that she took the motto and the title for her first full-length non-fiction book about her native town, *A Goodly Heritage,* which she describes as "an account of the traditions behind the formation of New England life and thought."[5] The book is a study in detail and in depth of Blue Hill—sufficiently in depth to reveal that the roots of the village culture were identical with the roots of the culture of the region and, indeed, of the nation. Miss Chase has never regarded her material to be of solely sectional interest; she insists that she writes of and for America as a whole.

A Goodly Heritage belongs to a prolific genre of New England and, especially, of Maine writing—a combination of local color and reminiscence—which includes works by Harriet Beecher Stowe, Celia Thaxter, Robert Tristam Coffin, Sarah Orne Jewett. Miss Chase admits a large debt to Sarah Orne Jewett, whom she had met during childhood and to whom she confided her own desire to write books, receiving the author's encouragement: "I'm sure you will, and good books, too, all about Maine." Miss Chase's admiration for Sarah Orne Jewett has never changed. In 1962 she wrote: "She is justly the master of us all.... Even the best among us distantly follow her footsteps, stumbling and fumbling among the words which she so perfectly set down on paper, among the people whom she so unerringly portrayed, among the marshes and islands, the coves, the hills, the villages which she saw with a vision denied to all other Maine authors."[6]

Whether Miss Chase's modesty is justified or not, in *A Goodly Heritage* she does a more thorough job than Miss Jewett, in uncovering the ingredients of the Maine way of life: a stable family, with a stern but just father and a loving and forgiving mother; a strict but enjoyable schooling; an eager awareness of nature; a vital religious life; a sense of oneness with the community; and plenty of laughter, which thirty years later Miss Chase is still able to share with her readers. The popularity of the book, which was immediate and lasting, results in part from its style, which is vivid and informal and good-naturedly ironic, and from the interesting and likable people who come alive on its pages. Yet, in a greater degree, its appeal must stem from the desire felt by so many moderns for exactly the emotional and intellectual security Mary Ellen Chase reports as being typical of village life in New England in the last century. So long as civilization teeters on the brink, as it has done through two world wars and a depression and is doing in the present nuclear arms race, this book will make seductive reading. But any one designating *A Goodly Heritage* as an escapist work is inaccurate. It does not transport the reader into a land that never did and never can exist; rather, it deals with what was once a norm, and is still a very real potential, in American life.

In writing *A Goodly Heritage,* as well as most of her other books, Mary Ellen Chase has associated herself with that impressive, though critically somewhat spurned, group of writers who insist on seeking and even finding positive values in our national culture in a period when it has become intellectually unfashionable to find anything but negative values. Undoubtedly the negative—the lost dreams, the despair, the crassness of spirit—exist; but perhaps the positive exist also, and have existed far back into American history. At least Mary Ellen Chase thinks so, as did so many of our authors of the past—Howells, Henry James, Hawthorne, Whitman. In our own century three or four women novelists other than Miss Chase have recorded a confidence in the moral and spiritual resources of the American character. These writers, among whom should be included Ellen Glasgow, Willa Cather, and Dorothy Canfield Fisher, may be called Humanists in that they regard humanity as possessing potentials of soul and mind not found in the rest of organic or inorganic nature. They are distinct from the Naturalists—Zola, Dreiser, Frank Norris—who regard man as part of, and not in any way outside of, the material universe.

A basic premise of these Humanist writers is that communities and individuals in America belong to a continuing tradition which the newness of our environment has too often caused us to overlook. An excellent early statement of this viewpoint is made by Sarah Orne Jewett in her preface to her first book, *Deephaven.* Following a train of thought suggested by words she had read in George Sand's preface to *Legendes Rustiques* Miss Jewett writes: "There will . . . exist that . . . class of country people who preserve the best traditions of culture and of manners, from some living inborn instinct toward what is simplest and best and purest, who know the best because they themselves are of kin to it. . . . Human nature is the same the world over, provincial and rustic influences must ever produce much the same effects upon character, and town life will ever have in its gift the spirit of the present, while it may take again from the quiet hills and fields and the conservatism of country hearts a gift from the spirit of the past."[7]

In the Maine coast hamlet described in her best work, *The Country of the Pointed Firs,* Sarah Orne Jewett discerned this persistent spirit of the past, an ageless dignity not unlike that of some ancient village of Greece or France or Italy. She directly compares the landscape to that of Greece; her sturdy heroine, Elmiry Todd, she likens to Antigone venting her grief on the plains of Thebes; and, in a country girl tending her sheep, she sees one of the timeless peasants on Millet's canvases. The comparisons are convincing, of course, only because the characters and scenes are convincingly portrayed. We can believe in the connections with the past only because we are certain of the reality of present people and events. Mary Ellen Chase, as we shall see later, makes similar use not only of Classical allusions but more extensively of Biblical references and comparisons to relate the people in her books to scriptural antiquity. Both women increase the stature of their people by relating them to an ancient tradition.

Willa Cather, following the timely advice of her friend Sarah Orne Jewett, turned from the production of sterilities in the Jamesian "international" vein and began a search for traditional values in the lives of immigrant-pioneers of her own Nebraska plains. The values she uncovered among these newcomers from Central and Northern Europe were analogous to those of her own Virginia and Presbyterian background and therefore with those of Calvinist New England: respect for hard work, personal integrity, loyalty to friends and family and ideals, humility, and self-reliance. Ellen Glasgow discovered the same vein of life-sustaining qualities among the back-country Virginia families from which she traced her own descent, and Dorothy Canfield Fisher found her Vermonters to be rich with similar spiritual wealth. These novelists are productive and artistically able, but, with the exception of Willa Cather, they have been rather neglected.

The works of these Humanistic writers express a faith not only in the durability of a tradition but also in the Emersonian law of compensation. Their probings strike deposits of spiritual and moral gold in the most unpromising environments—the run-out lands of Western Virginia, the economically by-passed coast of Maine, the flinty and thin-soiled valleys of the Green Mountains, the blizzard swept, sun-baked High Plains. The law of compensation, in its simplest terms, says that spirit transcends matter; out of defeat comes victory; out of ugliness, beauty; out of discouragement, courage.

The Maine coast during most of Miss Chase's lifetime has not afforded an easy or an affluent life. It has been an area where people must seek and live by compensations. The climate is cold from November to May, with abundant snow and icy rains. At all seasons week-long fogs make navigation a hazard and a misery. The land is predominantly cobblestone and granite, unfit for truly profitable farming. And even the granite which once was quarried and shipped in schooners and barges to Boston, New York, and farther is no longer in demand. The nearby waters, though abounding in lobster and herring, yield their bounty only with the utmost reluctance. Shipping, formerly the mainstay of most coastal families, has utterly vanished. Yet even on the economic level there are compensations. Some families eke out a hard and meager living from a string of lobster traps or a herring weir; others cut spruce for the paper mills; others go to work for the summer residents or set up a shop to catch some of the tourist trade. The best of the coast people, one way or another, rise above economic adversity; nor do they become embittered. Even those who seek a living elsewhere, as many do, return often and remain loyal to their old homes.

For the crowning compensation of all—the one that keeps the people on the coast and holds their loyalty all their lives even though they live afar—is the region's surpassing beauty which nullifies much of its harshness. Who could be insensitive to, or ignore, the blue-green mountains rolling up from the sea; the numerous bays that cut deeply into the spruce-forested mainland; the countless woody, surf-ringed islands strewn along the coast and spilling far to seaward? Who could forget the sea itself, clear and cold as a mountain stream, a sensitive mirror of the ever changing moods of the sky; or the brief, bright springs and summers and the incomparable autumns with their sparkling air, sharply etched lines of coast and mountain, and beneficent yellow sunshine? Always, above all, will be the vision, whether in memory or actuality, of the villages that nestle white and gleaming between the granite shores and the pastures. Here, though man struggles constantly *with* nature, he is at *one* with nature. He suffers from no sense of alienation. Sarah Orne Jewett and Mary Ellen Chase affirm that life may be hard here, but it is infinitely worth living. The coast may grant grudgingly the bodily necessities, but it is a doting mother in bestowing the gifts of the spirit on those who will accept them. As one author has put it, the Maine coast is a place for which one is homesick even when one is there.

III *True and Pleasant Words:* The White Gate

In 1954, twenty-two years after *A Goodly Heritage,* Mary Ellen Chase published another book on her girlhood in Blue Hill, *The White Gate,* aptly subtitled *Adventures in the Imagination of a Child.* Though dealing with the same general material and with many of the same episodes, this book is more analytic, more thoughtful, and more poetic than the earlier one. Into it she put her best efforts; for, as she confesses, it is not easy to translate one's past into "true and pleasant words."[8] Again the pervading theme corresponds to Alyosha Karamazov's belief that, for our spiritual health, we must be constantly fortified by memories of experiences in childhood. Again Miss Chase successfully demonstrates that growing up in a Maine village of sixty years ago furnishes a plethora of such experiences. And doubtless she is right. A homogeneous village which provides a secure and unchanging way of life, in which family solidarity remains unchallenged, in which church and school occupy unassailable but well-defined positions, and in which everyone knows everyone else and everyone knows exactly what is expected of him at any particular moment in any particular context—this is the obvious place for a happy childhood. Yet, even in such a favorable environment, every child above the vegetable level of intelligence and susceptibility must be from time to time beset with misgivings and fears. To be otherwise is not to share in the human lot. In none of her books has Miss Chase closed her eyes to the darker moments in a child's struggle for full awareness. But nowhere does she so dramatically contrast the lights and the shadows as in *The White Gate.*

In the Preface, Miss Chase describes the genesis of the book. For the May, 1951, issue of *The Ladies' Home Journal,* she had written an essay entitled "Recipe for a Magic Childhood." The next year the article, which aroused much interest, appeared as a little book, which in turn was so successful that her publishers urged her to write a longer book, primarily for children. But Miss Chase, although she had started her career as a writer of juveniles, now found herself unsuited for the task. As a girl she had not distinguished between children's and adults' books—between *The Mill on the Floss* and *Five Little Peppers,* or between *The Old Curiosity Shop* and *Little Women.* Nor was she, while writing *The White Gate,* able to demarcate literature by age level distinctly enough to enable her to write for just one age group. Yet she still wished to "recapture those vivid, if half-formed, impressions, those glimpses of reality and perceptions of wisdom, which in the long succession of dimly remembered days are in the life of the child like the flashing of fireflies in the darkness. For all of us as children... possess an instinctive capacity for wonder, for quick surprise, even for a puzzling sense of mystery, which redeems mere events in the beginning of our lives and which actually decides the wealth or the poverty of our later thoughts and, therefore, the nature of ourselves... [and we] weave by some secret, silent process strand by strand the spiritual pattern of our lives..." (10).

The doctrine is Rousseauean and Dostoyevskian; it is, to an even greater degree, Wordsworthian: "The child is father to the man...." Miss Chase's psychology is the semi-mystical one of the "Ode on Intimations of Immortality" and of "The Prelude." It is particularly Wordsworthian in that, as stated before, she describes not only the ecstasies but also the terrors of childhood. Wordsworth records the sudden numbing fear of the child at the cliff's edge or in the shadows that stalk along the moonlit river. These fears, which are associated with some guilty act, are as much a part of the child's spiritual development as are inklings of pre-existence described in the immortality ode.

In *The White Gate,* the terror, though not associated with guilt, is similarly indispensable to the child's growth. One summer, for example, the little girl went through a daily ordeal of fear when she went forth to fetch the family cow from a lonely wooded and shadow-haunted pasture some distance from her home. Also throughout her childhood and, with less frequency, in her adult years, she was recurrently terrorized by a nightmare in which she imagined herself lost in an unbounded, utterly silent plain of white salt-like crystals under a drifting pall of heavy white mist. Across the expanse she would trudge, leaving no footprints, sinking deeper and deeper at each step, until it seemed she would not be able to extricate herself and she would disappear beneath the surface. From this dream she would awaken screaming. Her parents would rush to her bedside to assure her, "It's all right. It's only a dream." "But," Miss Chase writes, "it was not all right then, nor has it ever been. And I've never been at all sure that it is only a dream" (99). When her parents let her have a room of her own, the fulfillment of a long-cherished ambition, her joy was spoiled by the fear of waking up from her nightmare without the comforting presence of the sisters with whom she had previously slept.

Persons, too, were sources of anguish. The gypsies, dark and gleaming-eyed, who occasionally came down the road in their caravans and stopped in front of the house, filled the children with panic. More profound was the feeling of pain and shame that she empathetically shared with her Uncle Roscoe when she first became aware that he was psychoneurotic. Uncle Roscoe, a paperhanger, suffered acute anxiety arising from his inability to achieve perfect matching of the flowers on the paper he sometimes had to hang on walls of houses hopelessly out of plumb. One day in her aunt's kitchen Mary Ellen was nursing a finger which she had painfully cut. Uncle Roscoe, returning for lunch, slumped into his chair without noticing the child, and hiding his face in his hands, moaned, "My God! More roses!" (68). Mary, in the throes of her own physical injury, was overwhelmed by the sudden recognition of the mental hurt of her uncle. Later she learned the psychiatric jargon applicable to her uncle's case—perfectionism, frustration, obsession. But, as a child, she was aware only of his agony and understood it better than most adults who would be prone to laugh at what on the surface appeared to be only a ridiculous idiosyncrasy rather than a life-blighting illness.

More than most of her works, *The White Gate* is strong in symbols. The most important is the gate itself in the white picket fence surrounding the family residence. As Miss Chase writes in her first chapter, this gate, which opens onto a road leading down a steep hill to the bay, is what separates her and her many brothers and sisters from the outer world. Standing at the gate, the children could glance back at "the sureness" of their home. Looking before them, they could see the excitement, the uncertainties that might "be coming or going along that road between the sky and the sea" (16). Their imagination fed avidly on what lay beyond the gate which gave access to the good and the bad, the true as well as the false; for the gate resembled those in Virgil's *Aeneid* of ivory and horn through which true and false dreams passed on their way up from Hades to the minds of men. This symbolism is not, of course, only a literary device. It is an instance of the actual symbolism that pervades the consciousness of every sensitive person—half-apprehended, perhaps, but very real.

Other symbols in *The White Gate* stand for specific experiences of deep import but inexplicable except by images—by the circumstances of their occurrence. Miss Chase describes such experiences in the chapter entitled "Two Days of Discovery." On one of the days, Mary is returning in bitter winter weather from an afternoon visit to a friend. Her body aches with cold and she wonders how she can endure until she arrives home. She weeps and the tears running down her cheeks congeal into pellicles of ice. Inexplicably—for her only desire is for the warmth of her mother's kitchen—she stops at a bridge over a brook that, despite the ice, gurgles happily along. Leaning against the railing and gazing down, she notices tiny animal tracks in the snow on either side of the brook. Engrossed by the delicate pattern of the footprints, she forgets the coldness. She does not interpret them either in words or in ideas. Yet "they became . . . in those moments a living experience, the entire content of a day, its reality, its only meaning" (118). When her father appears in a sleigh to pick her up and finds her still standing on the bridge, she resents him as an intruder.

The second "discovery" is even more intangible but not less real. As she is walking along the sidewalk on a misty morning, the sun suddenly breaks through with a light she had never seen before. She writes: "I felt as though I myself were filled with light and motion, as though I had never before been truly awake" (120). To use her term, she had undergone "a transfiguration." Such experiences Miss Chase later understood to be essentially mystical and much more commonplace than most of us, accustomed as we are to scientific or pseudo-scientific explanations of all phenomena, are willing to admit. It is part of the strength of Miss Chase's writing in this beautiful little book that she does not attempt to "explain" things. The feelings were experienced; they were connected with certain "real" facts—the tracks of field mice on the snow or a burst of sunlight on a foggy morning in spring. The feelings happened to her, and she tells us how and where they happened. This is all she can honestly do, and this is enough. To persons who have them, such experiences become the most important in their lives, Miss Chase believes; they stand at the source of all that supports us and provide meaning in later years. To use Miss Chase's favorite theological phrase, they are the outward visible signs of an inward spiritual grace—which is as good a definition of a symbol as one can reasonably ask for.

In all her works, Miss Chase recognizes that the inner growth of a child is secret and incommunicable. A child will instinctively conceal what is dearest and most significant to him. An example is Miss Chase's love of words. In several books, including *The White Gate,* she tells the fascinating part played by words in her childhood. The mother's imagination liked to toy with the idea of the special personality—color, tone, dignity or lack of it—of certain words, and the children entered into the game with glee. The father would recite from memory passages of literature whose sound happened to catch his ear. Her Uncle Henry, a searcher of polysyllables in the dictionary, would employ the ones he found with delightful but unconscious inappropriateness. In school the importance of words was emphasized by the constant drill in spelling and the competitive spelling bees. And in the church the minister had a way of reading the Bible so as to bring out all the color and music of its language, so that for the rest of her life Miss Chase associated certain passages with the memory of light streaming in the church windows or with the breathing of the wind on the meadows outside.

All the children shared in this gusto for language. But with Mary Ellen it was more than a gusto; it was a secret fascination, a passion—one which, like all passions, must be shielded from the gaze and comments of the world, even of one's own family. Thus when, at the age of twelve, she began a collection of words in a notebook purchased with money given her for her birthday, she concealed her hoard behind a rafter in a remote corner of the hayloft where it was never discovered. Here she would surreptitiously add to her verbal treasures, which she classified according to the mood they evoked: Sad words, such as *if, alone, stranger, solitary, shadowy;* glad words such as *radiant;* frightening words, like *darkness* and *death.*

Thus the child grows in spirit, imagination, and mind. Though the process goes on largely unseen, the results are uncovered year by year. An individual person, a being unlike any that ever existed or ever will exist again, emerges from the welter of heredity and environment, a product of these yet distinct from them, having roots in deeper regions than any yet plumbed by psychology or biology. If the germination is in beauty, the growth will be flourishing and hardy against the inevitable encroachments of ugliness and pain. This was the case with Mary Ellen Chase's childhood.

Her growing up, with its beginning in beauty, is represented—in fact, allegorized—in *The White Gate* in the chapter "The Birth of an Island." One May day, when the brook that flowed past her house was in freshet, she noticed a clump of grass caught onto a sprig of blossoming sugar pear—a favorite flower of hers—drifting down the current. As she watched, it brought up against some stones and tenaciously stuck there. Day after day she went to see if the frail cluster of twigs still remained, and it was always there—the germ of a new island. Months and years went by. The island grew, firmly rooted to the bottom and blooming with flowers of its own, until at last report, the time of the writing of *The White Gate,* it was twenty feet long, a firmly established, distinct piece of soil, separated from the rest of the earth by a narrow thread of isolating water.

"No man is an island," Donne meditated. This is true insofar as we all share in a common humanity. But, insofar as each of us is an inviolable, individual immortal soul, we are islands embraced in the arms of the life-giving waters. As our own characters and talents grow, we break away from our family, first perhaps by merely having a room of our own (the subject of another chapter in *The White Gate*); later, by passing through the white gate into the outer world, where we exist as separate entities in constant attraction and repulsion with the rest of mankind.

Some such things as these are what Miss Chase is saying in *The White Gate,* which is at once the sparsest but also the most suggestive and the most poetical book that she has written. She herself says she wrote it "purely for fun and got that fun, 'pressed down and running over.' "[9] Creativity is, of course, pure fun; and in no other book has Miss Chase's creativity been more in evidence. But the spirit of fun is the only appropriate one in which to write about childhood, even if one writes of the sorrows and fears, as well as the joys. And *The White Gate* stands as Miss Chase's ultimate word on childhood, always to her the most important of all subjects.

CHAPTER 2

A Teacher, Not an 'Educator'

IN 1939 Miss Chase published *A Goodly Fellowship,* the second of her autobiographical volumes. In her Preface she states that she wrote the book not only to satisfy friends who looked forward to a sequel to *A Goodly Heritage* but also, and more importantly, because she enjoyed writing it. The book, she explains, is to deal with teaching, which to her has always been the good life. She hopes that it will be of value to all who are interested in the changes in American education during the past thirty years. But, she warns, "I am a teacher not an 'educator,' and what I know of my job has been acquired not through experiment but through experience, not by theory but by practice" (xii).

Aside from being a valuable and interesting piece of autobiography, *A Goodly Fellowship* has been received, even by the "educators" whom she disowns, as a sort of classic statement of the ideals and practices of American education. Lyman Bryson, philosopher and professor at Columbia University Teachers College writes: "Mary Ellen Chase has not only her confidence in herself and in the democratic system; she has also, to a degree that might seem naïve in a person less learned and less wise, an unshaken faith in the efficacy of education, as she has seen it practiced in many forms, to save men and women and to build a civilization. In this she serves, involuntarily perhaps, as spokesman for the teachers of the United States, especially for the dominant group of women in the public schools who are the builders of the constantly renewed American foundation."[1]

This confidence in education, which is unquestionably basic in Miss Chase's outlook as a writer, was nowhere stronger than in the New England in which she grew up. To repeat, the church and school were dominant but coequal institutions in most New England towns and in most American towns deriving from New England; and both church and school were founded on faith in man's potential for personal salvation and for social and intellectual betterment. Any list of America's great teachers and educational theorists is liberally sprinkled with the names of New Englanders: Horace Mann, Bronson Alcott, Elizabeth Peabody, Mary Lyons, John Dewey.

I *What Makes a Good Teacher*

Mary Ellen Chase views successful teaching as a function of personality. Courses in "methods" she scorns as worse than worthless—a scorn that she shares with many professors in our liberal arts colleges. She congratulates herself on never having been subjected to a single such course. The greatest asset any teacher can have, she believes, is a consuming interest in his subject. This truth she learned as a girl from her mother, who reviewed her children's lessons with joy for herself as well as for the children. Her enthusiasm and vitality brought to life historical incidents, poems, and places that had been only inert matter in the schoolroom. On Saturday morning mother and daughter would churn butter to the leaping anapests of "The Assyrian came down like a wolf on the fold." Miss Chase writes that her "mother's imagination cast gleams and motes of light upon the worn pages of our school Speller" (9), to most pupils the least inspiring of all textbooks. She shared with her children her own feeling of "the charm and magic" of certain words like *multitude* and *meander;* and the "stupidity" of others, like *moreover*. Unconsciously the child was learning the fundamentals of literary style.

Good teachers, according to Miss Chase, must be exhibitionists, performers. They must be caught up by their subject, merged with it, as a good actor becomes the part he is acting. Through her dramatic reading of Lamb's *Tales From Shakespeare,* Mrs. Chase made characters live and evoked for her children the emotions the playwright intended. Always she encouraged the children to translate their learning into the language and actions of everyday living—to apply their knowledge of fractions to the cutting of pies, their geometry to the measuring of the area of flower beds and cubic footage of woodpiles. On Saturday nights she had the whole family enact scenes from history read to them first by their father: Pliny's death at Pompeii, or Leonidas' heroism at Thermopylae. Unconsciously Mrs. Chase was using the "project method" of progressive education; that is, she taught through "guidance and suggestion" (13). Miss Chase considers this the best way of teaching and asserts that all good teachers use it, though perhaps unknowingly. But the teachers' colleges fail in promoting it because their courses consist largely of pretentious jargon, usurping the place of honest and inspired teaching of the subject which the students must learn to love well enough to teach it to others. Good teachers are born, not made. The training colleges should concentrate on teaching *what,* not *how,* to teach.

The mother's love of books infected the children, particularly Mary Ellen, who became an inveterate reader. As she puts it, she was unwittingly preparing for graduate school while reading during the long hours that she rocked the cradle successively occupied by five younger brothers and sisters. Her skill as a cradle-rocker enabled her to keep the baby asleep for stretches as long as three hours, during which, as the months and years passed, she read Shakespeare, Thackeray, George Eliot, Dickens, the Brontës, Hawthorne, Cooper, and Robert Louis Stevenson, along with some less adult fare such as Louisa May Alcott. Even among the children's games a favorite was "authors," which Miss Chase considers educationally valuable: "It stamped upon our careless minds . . . the names of great pieces of literature; it stored up in our memories ineradicable pictures of great men and women—George Eliot with her brooch and her parted hair, the genial and wry smile of Oliver Wendell Holmes, the massive sad face of Carlyle. . . ."[2]

From her mother, then, Miss Chase learned that learning is an exciting adventure. From her father she learned that it is hard work, requiring laborious study and unflagging attention to detail. The father, a successful lawyer, was a perfectionist who provided an essential corrective to the enthusiasm generated by the mother. He presented his offspring with lengthy lists of historical dates for memorization; he drilled them mercilessly in arithmetic. His theory of education, Miss Chase writes in *A Goodly Fellowship,* was stark: "the harder a task, the more satisfaction in its accomplishment" (14). His praise, since he gave it only when it was truly earned, was something to treasure. His ideas concerning physical work were no less rigid. The children, girls as well as boys, all had their outside chores to do: feeding or harnessing the horses, driving the cow to pasture, tending the garden, and picking the apples. Such work not only had its own intrinsic dignity, the father thought, but also cleared one's mind and stabilized one's emotions.

The father was a lover of artistic and natural beauty. He delighted in reciting from memory page after page of Homer's hexameters or Burke's speeches. One anecdote about him is reminiscent of Emily Dickinson's father, who once summoned the townspeople to view a spectacular aurora by ringing the church bell, the usual fire alarm. Mr. Chase aroused his family one midnight and herded them down the stairs and out to the back field to see an outstanding display of northern lights. After ten minutes of silent watching he dismissed them to bed with the terse order: "Don't forget it" (19).

Obviously, to Miss Chase, teaching is not an activity to be relegated solely to the schools. It goes on continuously in the home and in the neighborhood. Thus among the most influential of her non-academic teachers were the far-traveled older women of the town, wives and widows of the old shipmasters, of whom her grandmother was one. In their voyages back and forth across the world they learned some valuable lessons which they were glad to impart to any of the village young people sensible enough to listen to them. One of these lessons was that of tolerance. These women had been sufficiently exposed to other civilizations—other religions, customs, values—to be able to see their own New England culture as only one of many and perhaps not the ultimate one at that. The example of this breadth of intelligence that develops from wide experience was later an obvious influence in Mary Ellen Chase's own decision to strike out for herself in the Middle West and later in Europe. To understand one's village, one must have lived in the world. Far from diminishing love of home, sojourns abroad give one the love for it that comes with understanding. Also from world-wide voyaging comes a second important lesson imparted by the sea captains' wives—a calm which forms as the residue of frequent exposures to danger. "These women . . . had been too often beset by Fear itself to worry over mere fears" (22).

In her formal schooling Mary Ellen Chase considers herself fortunate. In the Blue Hill schools, especially in the academy, the pupils, as we have seen, received a sound education administered humanely but with much hard work and drill. Her favorite subjects in the academy were Greek, Latin, and English, and of the teachers of these she writes with admiration and gratitude. On her instruction at the University of Maine, which she classes as undistinguished at that time, she is almost silent; but the acquaintance she made there with girls of one of the old ship-owning families opened to her a wealth of material that she put to good use in her novels some twenty years later. Of the professors at the University of Minnesota Graduate School, which she attended in the early 1920's, she writes nothing but praise. Their teaching, she thought, was a unique exception to the insufferably uninspired teaching in most American graduate schools. For eight professors at the University of Minnesota her admiration is unstinted: Elmer Edgar Stoll in Shakespeare, Oscar Ferkins in history of the drama, Frederick Klaeber in Anglo-Saxon, Kemp Malone in linguistics, Cecil Moore in eighteenth-century novel, Joseph Warren Beach in nineteenth-century novel, Carleton Brown in Medieval literature, and Joseph Thomas in creative writing. Combining knowledge with enthusiasm, those men not only prepared their students to teach their chosen subjects but made them eager to do so.

II *Teaching in Schools*

Miss Chase's account of her own teaching, told with vividness, an abundance of anecdotes, and much humor, is of course the core of *A Goodly Fellowship*. Between her sophomore and junior years in college, she began teaching at the age of nineteen in a Maine one-room district school. Her father believed that three terms of rural-school teaching as an interruption in one's college course was invaluable in strengthening one's learning powers, enhancing one's endurance and ingenuity, and developing one's latent abilities. Miss Chase's story of her jobs in the tiny communities of Buck's Harbor and West Brooksville, within a few miles of Blue Hill, is one of the high points in her book. Hardly more than a child herself, she faced and subdued a room full of fishermen's sons and daughters whose idea of a frolic was to eject their teacher bodily from the schoolhouse. But Miss Chase was not ejected. Not only did she subdue them, by sheer bravado rather than by force of character, but she organized them, forty strong and spread through half a dozen grades, into a sort of endless belt of pupils that passed by her desk for processing in various branches of knowledge appropriate to their age and level. It was a situation in which any normal-school training in "methods" would have been a handicap. Improvisation alone was called for, and God help the faint-hearted and unresourceful teacher. But Miss Chase proved resourceful and efficient. When she returned to Orono to finish her college course, she taught English part-time to students of agriculture.

A teacher's first assignment is always the hardest, but it is doubly hard when one starts in conditions like those of Miss Chase's first job. Her success in the one-room school, which she ascribes as much to luck as to her own efforts, gave her the confidence for her later career in larger schools in the Middle and Mountain West and finally in college. Of her Western experiences we can allude to only a few in any detail. In 1909, having graduated from the University of Maine with a bachelor's degree, Mary Ellen Chase decided after much wavering and much family consultation to try her teaching fortunes in Chicago. The spirit of her seafaring ancestors was in her; to a Maine girl even of today Chicago seems almost beyond the bounds of civilization. But once there, she went on even farther, to Spring Green, Wisconsin, where she obtained a position at the Hillside Home School. Her stay there was one of the most enriching periods of her life and was important in the formation of her lifelong ideals of education. The school was directed by the Lloyd-Jones sisters, relatives of Frank Lloyd Wright, who himself lived in Spring Green and who had designed one of the school buildings. At Hillside the two sisters, who were born teachers, achieved—because of their combined common sense and idealism—the aims of progressive education while avoiding its many ludicrous mistakes. Like Miss Chase's mother they instinctively knew how to interest the young not only in learning but in the permanent values of living—cooperation, consideration, self-reliance, the joys of accomplishment.

The Lloyd-Joneses, as described by Miss Chase, make one think of the Transcendentalists, and they were indeed imbued with the thought of Theodore Parker, Channing, and Emerson. A love and an understanding of nature were the cornerstones of their curriculum. The school was no more than a large farm in a fertile, peaceful valley. Bird-watching and botanizing became almost substitutes for religious instruction. Sleigh-rides and nut-gathering expeditions were joyful pilgrimages. Work was treated as a duty, a pleasure, a form of worship. Each child had his own garden plot to plant, tend, and harvest; and, in addition to caring for his own room and personal belongings, each was assigned chores on the farm and in the school buildings.

That the Maine-coast girl should be attracted to and become an asset to a school like this is not surprising. Her own home life, with its values of self-reliance, responsibility, and versatility, was precisely the right and only training for a teacher at Hillside. The school in fact was a home, as its name implied, a family of many members, where the needs and abilities of each were the first consideration of all; where all shared in the benefits and the labor of the common life together. As Miss Chase says, "Ellen and Jane Lloyd-Jones were themselves country children. They realized . . . the infinite resources for the nourishment and cultivation of the human mind and imagination which such a condition of life may hold within itself if only its potentialities are understood" (104).

The right of self-expression was taken for granted at Hillside Home School, as it should be in any harmonious family. For example, each child in turn had the responsibility of saying meal-time grace. The choice was his—a Biblical passage, a stanza from a hymn, a short poem. Some of the selections were, of course, bizarre. But respect for the individual's right to choose and for the solemnity of the occasion precluded all chance that any choice be laughed at.

"What boys and girls learned from their books at Hillside," Miss Chase wrote, "became inevitably related to the life which they lived and to the companionship which they enjoyed and trusted" (115). What are some of the values usually purveyed by books but too frequently ignored even in the schools that teach them? Tranquillity of mind and spirit is surely one of the most widely preached and most seldom practiced. At Hillside tranquillity was inculcated by the observance of a five-minute period of total silence in the daily assemblies of students and faculty. No one even thought of breaking the silence because it had become an accepted part of daily existence, as regular and indespensable as meals. Another value more readily preached than practiced is kindness. At Hillside any cruelty to an animal or to another person, whether on the part of a pupil or a teacher, brought upon the offender the fury and contempt of the sisters. And so it went. Thoughts and ideals were translated into actions, and actions into thoughts—the reciprocating process that constitutes all true wisdom and education. The effect of Hillside on Mary Ellen Chase was permanent: "We traveled much in realms of gold at Hillside, saw many goodly sights of the earth, entered into many goodly kingdoms of the mind. Whatever vision or imagination I have been able to give to my teaching in the years since then, I owe to two women in a Wisconsin valley thirty years ago...." (121).

An almost mystical reverence for the human mind and personality was beginning to dominate Mary Ellen Chase's outlook at this time. A strong influence at Hillside was the sisters' Unitarianism with its Emersonian belief in the oversoul and the latent divinity of each individual. One lived virtuously because to do so was to live according to the God within one. Though Miss Chase was never a Unitarian theologically, this side of its doctrine, as observed at Hillside, was doubtless in harmony with her own trend of thought and may well have fortified it. At any rate, Miss Chase had small regard for the shallower virtues, those practiced not for their own sake but for reasons of social expediency or for furtherance of self.

After leaving Hillside, she taught in Chicago at a fashionable girls' school where the headmistress, a Miss Moffat, pretentiously stressed the ideal of duty to God and society, ignoring other values or virtues. Miss Chase quickly concluded that duty, as Miss Moffat interpreted it, was one of the most highly overrated qualities. For the "duty" that the headmistress harped on was simply a stimulus for incessant and frequently pointless action; it had no roots in the spirit; it reflected no religious convictions profounder than those of Rotarianism.

While teaching at Miss Moffat's school, Mary Ellen Chase was herself seeking philosophic foundations for the convictions about life and God that had been growing in her ever since she went to Hillside. Already ambitious to earn a doctor's degree, she was taking a course in philosophy in Chicago University under Professor Talbert, who lived in a world entirely different from Miss Moffat's. He revealed to his pupil the possibilities of a purely spiritual life, a revelation for which she still remembers him with gratitude. He was to her a living proof of the truth of two books that he introduced her to—William James's *The Varieties of Religious Experience* and Rudolf Eucken's *The Life of the Spirit.*

In 1913 Mary Ellen Chase took a summer off from Miss Moffat's school to go to Europe to study German, a language which she had already studied at the University of Maine. Here she encountered two teaching methods which represented two pedagogical extremes. The first was by a Prussian, Fräulein Franke, in Berlin, who motivated her students by making them hate her. Her chief teaching aids were a sarcastic tongue, a viperous temper, and a heavy, three-cornered pencil which served the dual purpose of making slashing corrections on her pupils' exercise books and whacking their knuckles, whether they were adults or not. Taking lessons from her was a battle for survival, the chief weapons being pride and self-respect. Anyone lacking in these qualities soon succumbed. Those who had them in sufficient strength to survive for several months learned German. Miss Chase endured this brutality as long as she had originally planned to stay in Berlin, but she regarded Fräulein Franke with anger and abhorrence mingled with pity.

From Berlin she went to the Harz Mountains, to the tutelage of three kindly and gracious Fräuleins who received in their home foreigners wishing to improve their German. Life there was an idyl of eating, cheerful conversation, and blissful walks among the hills, followed by evenings of group-singing of hymns and of sorrowful German songs, and oral readings from Hans Christian Andersen. Here was a German manifestation of the same spirit that ruled in the Hillside Home School. Miss Chase writes: "All things good and wholesome were in *das Elterhaus.* Merriment and sadness met there together as in all well-ordered homes. I shall never go back to Blankenburg; but I shall know it always as possessing a corner of this earth where people were born again in spirit" (164).

III *Montana: Reading and Meditation*

In 1914, after the death of her father at the end of a terrible illness, Miss Chase discovered that she was suffering from tuberculosis. Later she believed that this turn in her life was very fortunate; it forced upon her a year of rest, reading, and meditation in the Rocky Mountains of Montana. Her days and nights she spent out-of-doors in the high sparkling air. She continued her study of German; she returned to her Greek and Latin, as to long-slighted friends. Sometimes the cold forced her to hold her book in mittened hands, but she read Dante, Plato, the metaphysical poets, *The Brothers Karamazov, Anna Karenina, The Mayor of Casterbridge, Madame Bovary.* Never had she read the imperishable books more profoundly. Never had she been able to think about them so excitingly and let them settle so indelibly into her being. As she lay on her cot at night under the September constellations, she could feel "the common pulse" by which all nature is timed and could sense "the roll of the world eastward and watch [her] steady progress through the stars" (176). For the first time she understood Yeats's statement, "We begin to live when we have conceived life as a tragedy," not as a pessimistic thought, "but rather as a bright one, touched with humanity, filled with pity and understanding, embracing the world with wisdom" (178).

That winter she wrote her first book, though as far back as 1909 she had written pieces for juvenile magazines. A dozen ideas for novels were stirring within her mind, but, afraid of her own immaturity, she set herself to writing a children's story. She has always felt that her decision was right; one who has lived only twenty-eight years rarely has the experience to write a serious novel. However, on the day on which her first volume for girls, *His Birthday,* was accepted by the Pilgrim Press in Boston, which paid her $150 for it, she "sincerely believed that the world of literary achievement and success lay at [her] feet!" (179). As she says in her dedication, she had arrived at the "foothills of her promised land." There quickly followed *The Girl from the Big Horn Country,* obviously making use of her Montana experience, but, as she put it, this work was as undistinguished as the first. As a result, perhaps, of her own modest efforts, she now became fascinated with style. She eagerly read and attempted to imitate the great essayists—Lamb, De Quincey, Hazlitt, Pater—who remained life-time admirations. Their diction and the rhythms of their sentences, some of which she memorized, filled her with "a passion of excitement and wonder" (182). To her, she discovered, prose meant more than poetry. As in her childhood, she found she could still be bewitched by words—"their choice and combination, their sound and color, their height and depth, the possibilities within them of rhythm and movement" (183). She made her decision that she would devote her life to the teaching—not of philosophy, as she had hitherto planned—but of English prose.

To complete the recovery of her health, Mary Ellen Chase remained two more years in Montana, at Bozeman, not as an invalid but as a teacher in a public high school. Her students, with few exceptions, were rough, healthy, totally uninterested in books, but rich in kindliness and vitality. From them Miss Chase learned more than she was able to teach them. They imparted to her, by the mere presence of their robust bodies and glowing spirits in her classroom, a realization of what Emerson called the infinitude of the private man—"the sense," as Miss Chase puts it, "of basic, untutored natural excellence—in other words, a sense of those virtues and values which in the early ages of the world, when other lands were new, marked out gods and heroes and made them immortal in art and song" (192). By these boys and girls from the Montana ranches she was given new evidence of the timelessness and placelessness of human dignity, a concept fundamental to her life and writing and indispensable to any teacher, unless he be a hypocrite.

When the Montana school children brought to Miss Chase's mind the gods and heroes of ancient cultures, she was not succumbing to romantic delusion. She did not regard them as uncut diamonds or as noble savages. Rather, she appraised them in the light of the same Virgilian tradition of the heroic that illuminates Willa Cather's depiction of pioneer farmers and priests as founders and cultivators, not as destroyers. Those who till the soil, make the wilderness bloom, bring schools and churches to an uninhabited land are the heroes out of which the folk gods are made. If this was true in the age about which Hesiod, Homer, and Virgil wrote, it must be equally true today. By such people are civilizations founded, and about them is great literature written.

IV *Minnesota: Graduate School and College Teaching*

In 1917 Miss Chase at last left Montana to enter the University of Minnesota to prepare herself for teaching English in colleges. Mention has already been made of her admiration for her teachers there who she felt were so superior to those in most American graduate schools. Not only did they strengthen her knowledge of literature but they stimulated her love of it. To support herself her first year at the University, she wrote multitudinous articles for a number of Sunday-school journals on such subjects as the origins of words and the meanings of baptismal names. Her second year at Minnesota she became a part-time instructor in freshman composition. In addition to carrying half the normal load of graduate studies, she now taught twelve hours, read ninety student themes each week. No one who has not experienced it can quite imagine the rigors of such a life. Yet Miss Chase thrived on it and held, probably correctly, that this arrangement was more valuable to her than full-time study. She was learning as she taught, and learning and teaching contribute to each other. Also, since she had to fight for time for her studies, she valued them the more highly. With seven years of school-teaching and a serious illness behind her, the five years at Minnesota were the fulfillment of a cherished ambition. That they exacted from her the best of her powers of mind and character could only add to their joy. Complaint or self-pity would have been a betrayal of a cardinal principle of her Maine upbringing—nothing worth having ever comes easily.

In 1922 Miss Chase passed her oral examinations and received her doctor's degree. Her dissertation, written under the direction of Joseph Warren Beach, was entitled *Thomas Hardy from Serial to Novel;* the University of Minnesota Press published it in 1927. In it Miss Chase compares the serial and book versions of Hardy's three greatest novels: *The Mayor of Casterbridge, Tess of the D'Urbervilles,* and *Jude The Obscure.* The job needed to be done, for there are very marked differences between the versions of these works. Miss Chase's comparisons are painstakingly thorough; more than half the text consists of plot summaries and extended quotations. Her conclusions are unquestionably sound. The periodicals bowdlerized Hardy's novels since their editors were unwilling to risk shocking public opinion. In the book form, Hardy simply restored what the editors had jettisoned. Other differences that occur in the book versions are improvements that any artist would try to make in reprintings of his work: substitution of specific and vivid words for general and vague ones; correction of grammar; heightening of the Wessex atmosphere by more frequent use of place names; polishing of characterization.

Miss Chase's study of Hardy's style and technique and of his habits of revision was undoubtedly beneficial to her as a beginning writer. As so often happens with doctoral candidates, she ended by idolizing the subject of her thesis. To her, Thomas Hardy is the outstanding realist among English novelists, the most expert in plot and form, and the most philosophically significant—in other words "the greatest." Similarities to Hardy can be found in her own novels, not so much as a result of imitation as of genuine admiration and, above all, of certain elements in her background and her outlook. Hardy's use of nature as a gigantic impersonal stage setting, dwarfing his characters by its mere presence, would appeal to one used to the spaciousness of the Maine coast and the Western Plains and to the grim weather of both. At any rate Hardy's interest in nature and its effect on man and his detailed descriptions of it are echoed in Miss Chase's own novels. Similarly, Miss Chase's sense of destiny, her frequent use of strokes of fate—a sudden accident or catastrophe—are suggestive of Hardy.

Miss Chase stayed on at the University of Minnesota as an assistant professor for four years after getting her degree. To the present day she is happy that she had these years of teaching at a large state university before joining the staff of an exclusive Eastern girls college. In her classes at Minnesota were boys and girls of all social levels and ethnic and cultural backgrounds. She was particularly fond of the handsome, energetic, and ambitious Scandinavians from the villages and farms. To help them develop minds worthy of their bodies seemed eminently worth while.

Like many young professors Miss Chase augmented her income by teaching a night class in the university extension. The course, which was in creative writing, provided her with amusement, which is reflected in the humorous story, "Taxi Driver 63" (*Delineator*, February, 1936). But also the course deepened her understanding of writing as a profession. The tired office-workers, housewives, clergymen, plumbers, taxi drivers, and society women enrolled in her classes were for the most part rather devoid of talent and cared nothing for writing as an art. They were fired with one ambition—to see their names in print, even if only in a seed catalogue as happens in the comic piece, "Mrs. Penlust on the Damascus Road" (*Atlantic Monthly*, October, 1932). When Mrs. Penlust, whose distinction in the class is the fact that she is the only student with a complete lack of talent, finally sees her story "Bleeding Hearts" printed in a seed catalogue, she experiences the transports of the mystics.

Yet Miss Chase does not belittle the aspiration of these would-be authors. Their unrealizable dreams she considers worth while in themselves. They should not, however, be confused with the dreams of the professional, the artist, whose ideal must of necessity be mastery of his craft. Yet her students' goals and hers served to give life a purpose. "Life is tolerable," she writes, "only when some flame burns within one; and if it is kept burning, as I believe it is, in many minds and spirits through the opportunities afforded by University Extension Divisions, then power and glory be unto them from this time forth and even forevermore" (225).

Another of Miss Chase's teaching experiences while she was in Minnesota made a deep impression on her. During her last three years there she taught a class in advanced composition in the Roman Catholic College of St. Catherine, then on the outskirts of St. Paul. In graduate school she had become acquainted with one of the nuns on the faculty of St. Catherine, and she first visited the college as her guest. From the beginning, the life of the nuns was a marvel and an inspiration to Miss Chase. Paradoxically, their vows of self-denial seemed only to have enriched their lives. They were gay, humorous, scholarly, and energetic far beyond most lay people. They seemed to be extracting the fullest value from existence. Thus Miss Chase was delighted to be asked in 1923 to teach a class there and to share, if only partially, in this meaningful and rewarding life. The nuns' way of blending religion with work, prayer and devotions with cooking, teaching and gardening reminded Mary Ellen Chase of her own childhood home where the practical and the spiritual, the material and the moral merged indistinguishably in the daily and hourly routine. The Christianity of the convent, like that of her New England village, refused to divorce itself from even the drabbest of everyday concerns.

Miss Chase writes that St. Catherine's gave much more to her than she to it. What it gave her was a chance to satisfy the strongest thirst of her nature—the chance to pursue her livelihood, her chosen profession of teaching, in conjunction with the life of the spirit. Any life that fails to achieve this union falls short of fullest realization: if there is any single principle that pervades all of Mary Ellen Chase's work, both in teaching and in writing, this is it.

Not only did Miss Chase teach at the convent and visit there often, but she lived in it three summers almost as one of the nuns. As at Hillside Home School, she loved the friendliness, the sense of working together in the daily round of chores, above all the blessing of silence. To Mary Ellen Chase silence, one of the rarities of modern life, is an indispensable condition for spiritual health and growth. At Blue Hill, along the shore and in high, stony pastures back from the sea, she had first known the beneficence of stillness. At Hillside School, she had found it again in the periods of quiet at assembly; and the repose of the Montana valleys had fed her spirit. Describing, with her knack for simile and Biblical allusion, a visit to St. Catherine's many years later, she writes: "The two sounds which always bring St. Catherine's back to me were still there: the silence, which there is sound, and the quick, subdued, diligent tread of many footsteps moving always hither and yon upon the Lord's business. They always have made me think of those footsteps upon the mountains in Isaiah, bringing good tidings and publishing peace" (242-43).

V *Smith College*

In 1926 Mary Ellen Chase left the University of Minnesota and St. Catherine's College for a teaching position at Smith College in Northampton, Massachusetts. Here she has remained to the present day, though she retired from full-time teaching in 1955. For almost forty years she has lived in a typical New England colonial-style house on elm-lined Paradise Road just off the campus. With her during most of these years has lived Eleanor Shipley Duckett, an Englishwoman still a British subject, who before retirement taught Classical languages and literature in the college and is a specialist in Anglo-Saxon saints and in Latin writers of the Dark Ages. The friends share not only a love for Latin and Greek. Miss Chase in her essays and novels from 1927 onward displays an interest in conventual life, which she had of course become acquainted with in Minnesota, and in the Saints, especially those of the early English church, that were Miss Duckett's chief enthusiasm. With Miss Duckett also, Mary Ellen Chase yearly visited England, frequently traveling on foot through most of the counties north and south, but especially in Cambridgeshire and East Anglia and in Miss Duckett's own West Country. These English sojourns continue to the present day, for England has become a second home for Miss Chase with ties only less strong than those of New England.

At Smith Miss Chase made her reputation both as a writer and as one of the outstanding teachers of her generation. In Montana she had decided that her life would be spent in teaching English prose. The years in Minnesota were a preparation for this. The return to New England, which she had always planned on, brought quick fulfillment. Her last chapter in *A Goodly Fellowship* is a paean to the English teacher's profession, which she considers both the most difficult "teaching in the world to do and . . . more fun to do than anything else in the world" (267). No good teacher of English, she thinks, ever really knows just what he is teaching—an art, a language, philosophy, history, theology. Nor does he ever really know just how he should teach. Each class hour, each class group is a challenge to his understanding and ingenuity. Admittedly she loved best her chosen subjects: the English novel, the great essayists, and the English Bible. But unlike many scholarly teachers, who often have the temperaments of prima donnas, she did not think that her scholarship was demeaned by her teaching beginning courses to freshmen; and since President William Allan Neilson, who to Miss Chase was the ideal college president, correctly thought that freshmen deserve the most experienced professors, she always had her classes of first-year girls. Her main task was to teach them to read and to write, neither of which the majority did very well. Nor did she condescend to these younger students by assigning them easy readings. Rather she indulged her own tastes—one of the luxuries of English teaching, she writes—by assigning her favorite works, especially from Greek drama. No matter on what level, she regarded her teaching as a "companionship in literature" (279). Her chief aim has always been to bring her students to the knowledge "that all art is . . . creative, that one mind creates in another perhaps even a greater abundance than was in its own, and that in this sense the reader becomes an artist together with the writer" (280).

Doubtless Miss Chase had a similar aim in her public lecturing, in which she has engaged extensively from coast to coast down to the present day. Her audiences have been women's clubs, high school commencement gatherings, parents' organizations. Her subjects have been numerous and varied: "The Background of Maine for a Writer," "The Book of Job," "Symbolism in the Old Testament," "The Larger Life in Books," "Sarah Orne Jewett," "Thomas Hardy," "The More Intelligent Reading of Fiction," to name but a few. In taking to the road as a lecturer, she was following a tradition established by some of America's greatest writers: Thoreau, Whitman, Twain, and Emerson. Like them, she earned money, added to her own knowledge, and widened her reputation. But her chief motive, she writes, was that she enjoyed lecturing; for lecturing is a form of teaching; and teaching, Miss Chase insists, is her first profession. But it has also been an essential stimulant to her as a writer. Lecturing, she found, brought her into contact with the larger world outside the college campus, it carried her to distant or out-of-the-way places, and it gave her opportunities for travel by railroad, of which she is particularly fond. Above all, lecturing gave her a vision of America, a nation that she feels holds "many sure and certain glimpses of eternal life" (261).

CHAPTER 3

The Foothills of the Promised Land

I The Art of Narration

WHILE still at the University of Minnesota, Mary Ellen Chase collaborated with a fellow teacher, Frances K. Del Plaine, on a textbook for college students, *The Art of Narration*. In her part of it, Miss Chase put much of what she had learned from teaching her classes in creative writing. But she was also drawing from personal experience, and success, as well; for by that time she had published not only three children's novels but also three short stories in *Harper's* and one each in *Atlantic Monthly* and in *Scribner's*. Also, at that time her first serious novel, *Uplands*, had just been completed, for it too was published in 1926. *The Art of Narration*, then, must reflect her own working ideas.

The book consists of twelve sections, each on a different type of narrative and each containing a brief introduction followed by extensive illustrative selections. Of these introductions Miss Chase wrote six; those to "Historical Narrative," "Historical Fiction," "Tales and Legends," "Biographical Narrative," "Narrative of Adventure," and "Stories." Miss Del Plaine was in charge of "Expository Narrative," "Incident," "Fairy Tales," "Allegories," "Parables," "Fables," "Reminiscent Narrative," "Narrative of Travel," and "Sketches." There is no reason to suppose that each was not in agreement with the tone and purport of the other's ideas, and indeed the book is consistent in its instruction and progresses in an orderly fashion. Both authors continually hammer home three main points. First, the would-be writer, whenever possible, should use materials from his own life and background—family, race, locality, nationality. Second, narrative, whether fictional or not, is potentially didactic, that is, a means of purveying information. Third, concrete and specific detail is the lifeblood of any narrative writing.

The fullest discussion of the use of personal experience is in Miss Del Plaine's introduction to "Reminiscent Narrative," and what she says applies perfectly to Miss Chase's later writings in that genre. Out-of-the-way places and their customs, Miss Del Plaine states, are excellent material for reminiscence. As an example she aptly cites Hudson's *Far Away and Long Ago,* a work close in style and spirit to Miss Chase's autobiographical books. In the United States, Miss Del Plaine continues, there are numerous distinct localities with characteristics of their own that would be of interest to readers from elsewhere. Obviously, the Maine coast is such a locality.

Miss Chase, in her comments on "Stories," is most specific concerning the didactic qualities of narrative. There are two kinds of narrative, she asserts: artistic and informational. Yet even the artistic story conveys information. The purpose of serious fiction, in the words of Bliss Perry, is "to show why certain people do certain things under certain circumstances." Plot is important in stories, but it is not so important as the revealing of motivation and, particularly, the effect of environment on action and personality—so much the preoccupation of Miss Chase's favorite novelist, Thomas Hardy. In other words, stories demonstrate why persons act as they do; they are lessons in human behavior. She very appropriately includes Willa Cather's *The Sculptor's Funeral* as an illustrative piece.

In introducing "Narratives of Adventure" Miss Chase most fully develops the principle of concreteness. As a chief example, she uses selections from Pierre Loti's *Iceland Fishermen,* a book in which many a Maine Coast fisherman has recognized his own life. She has the highest praise for Loti's use of detail in describing life and work on shipboard and, above all, for his descriptions of the sea and his evocation of its moods. Effective description, she emphasizes, and convincing atmosphere depend on the choice of image-making words to depict a limited number of carefully selected details.

The Art of Narration does not, to be sure, suggest any startlingly new devices. It seems, in fact, quite conventional and traditional, especially after nearly forty years of change in the art of story writing. But for the most part, Miss Chase has not been an experimenter. To her a serviceable style is one which conveys images and meanings clearly. She has gone on record as being opposed to the more difficult prose writing of our day, especially when it approaches obscurantism. As P. H. Boynton has pointed out, her own material and her purposes do not call for innovation.[1] But neither does she write in the expository style so common in nineteenth-century fiction. She is writing narrative, not exposition; her characterizations, dialogue, description, and plots progress under their own momentum with a minimum of supporting commentary. *The Art of Narration,* however, serves as a helpful, if not exhaustive, introduction to Miss Chase's fiction.

II *First Short Stories*

Of Sarah Orne Jewett's *The Country of the Pointed Firs* Mary Ellen Chase has written that it was "my ideal when I began to try to write. So far as that ideal goes, it has never lost its secure place."[2] The groping for this ideal is discernible in her first serious attempts at fiction—short stories written for *Harper's Magazine.* The presentation of rural values, characters, and settings is their chief function, as it is with Miss Jewett's stories. The style is simple and direct, like Miss Jewett's, but the dialogue does not succeed so well in catching the cadences and the diction of Maine speech. The atmosphere, too, suffers in comparison to Miss Jewett's in that it is not localized; it is obviously rural, but neither distinctly coastal nor inland. The breath of the sea and the scent of the firs, as well as the details of maritime life, are lacking. Nor is there any hint of Miss Chase's later consuming interest in the seafaring tradition of the coastal towns.

In its theme and in its use of childhood memories, however, her very first story for adults (she had written juvenile stories earlier), "A Return to Constancy," which appeared in the November, 1918, issue of *Harper's,* presages much of Miss Chase's later writing. A reader of her autobiographical books and essays would immediately recognize the cow Constancy, on whose name the title of the story puns. She is the same amiable, though individualistic, bovine that the Chase children drove back and forth to pasture in the 1890's. The point of the tale is essentially that of the later accounts: the relationship between an animal and a child can be of priceless, though intangible, worth. In the story the girl Cynthia rebels against her duties with Constancy; but, after a trip to Augusta with her father, she sees things differently. The daily treks to the pasture have made her intimate with the natural loveliness in which she lives—the plants and trees and flowers, the meadows, and the varying seasons. The cow herself has been a companion, though at times an exasperating one, from whom she has learned much, not only about animal nature but also about her own capacities for faithfulness and perseverance. Cynthia's return home from Augusta, where the governor's wife, with whom she had dined, implores her not to cease her duties with the cow, is indeed a "return to constancy."

Miss Chase's second story, "Sure Dwellings," published in *Harper's* the following year, is also an account of a return to the security of the place of one's roots. In subject, if not in theme, it anticipates her books about the clergy—her biography, *Jonathan Fisher, Maine Parson;* and the novel *The Lovely Ambition.* In the story a rural minister is invited to visit, all expenses paid, a celebrated New York City clergyman who has summered in the country parson's Maine community. The contrast between the wordly prosperity, the suavity, the theological modernism of the one and the awkwardness and traditionalism of the other is done with feeling; and this work hints at Miss Chase's later concern with the rift between "summer people" and "natives" on the Maine coast. In the city the visitor from Down East, with his unmodish dress and ignorance of urban ways, is placed in one humiliating position after another. The conference of ministers, at which he had hoped to read his treatise on baptism by immersion, fails to avail itself of that edifying pleasure. When he is invited to improvise a prayer before his host's Fifth-Avenue congregation, he finds himself without inspiration and can only stammer a series of disconnected clichés. The agony of his visit is fortunately cut short by an emergency that calls him back to his Maine parish. During his first prayer in his own church his inspiration returns, and he finds security and purposefulness in the "sure dwellings" of the Lord. Miss Chase passes no judgment. The country parson is rather pitiable; his city colleague, though lacking in understanding, is not arrogant. There is simply a wall between the two—perhaps between the two ways of life—which is not to be breached.

Miss Chase's third story, "Marigolds," also appearing in 1919, is the last of her early efforts that we shall discuss in any detail. It tells of a woman's love of flowers and her feelings of guilt when she pulls up some of her husband's vegetable seedlings and plants marigolds in their place. When her husband stupidly attributes the flowers to the vagaries of the government, which had sent him the vegetable seeds in the first place, her guilt diminishes; and it is entirely dispelled by the un-Puritanical thought, "No one is punished for joy."[3] The clash between the beauty-loving wife and the insensitive husband who begrudges her a square foot of land for her flowers recalls Mary Wilkins Freeman's famous "Revolt of Mother," and the finicky conscience of the wife is suggestive of Mrs. Freeman's many psychological studies of guilt-ridden New Englanders. All three of these stories, as well as others that followed in the next ten years, place an emphasis upon the limitations and compensations of village life. They are as much in the vein of the realistic local color practiced by Mary Wilkins Freeman and Rose Terry Cooke as in the more idyllic vein of Sarah Orne Jewett. What distinguishes them from the work of all Miss Chase's predecessors is the gently ironic objectivity that marks the style of much of her best writing.

Miss Chase has written surprisingly few short stories, and the ones she has written are sketches and vignettes rather than plotted narratives. Most of them could—and some did, in modified form—serve as essays or episodes in her autobiographical writings. Her most obvious success was the O. Henry-like story, "Salesmanship," which won $1,500 in 1937 in a contest sponsored by *The Pictorial Review.* Her notable work in fiction, however, has been in the novel. Her first book in that genre, *Mary Christmas,* was published by Little, Brown and Company in 1926.

III Mary Christmas

In the *White Gate* (1954) Miss Chase has told how profoundly the Maine villagers feared and distrusted the swarthy peddlers, Gypsies or Armenians, who tramped the summer roads at the turn of the century. And in a book of essays, *The Golden Asse* (1929), she deplores the blank spot resulting from the lack of saintlore in the lives of Protestant New England children. *Mary Christmas* owes its existence to these two impressions of her girlhood at Blue Hill. The Armenian peddler Mary Christmas brings to the village its first acquaintance with the saints at the same time that she makes a major dent in its xenophobia. For both accomplishments the townspeople who know her best are deeply grateful.

Mary Christmas makes her strongest impact on the Wescott family, the Chase family in transparent disguise. Mr. Wescott, the town magistrate, had befriended Mary when she was arrested and was brought before him for no other reason than that her "foreign" appearance had frightened some exceptionally timid farm folk. Lawyer Wescott not only quickly dismisses the case but invites the defendant to his house for lunch. Thus a lifelong friendship begins. The Wescott children, two boys and two girls, are immediately and totally enslaved by the dark woman with her red silk kerchief and gold-coin earrings. Never have they seen eyes so expressive as hers; they gleam with hate or swim in sorrow as she relates the wrongs and sufferings endured by her fellow Armenians at the hands of the Turks. Never in their Yankee village have they witnessed such untrammeled violence of feeling, or heard the word *kill* used with such abandon and gusto. To American children living before the two world wars, her life's story is a lurid one: her husband butchered by the oppressors; her children living in their native land awaiting the time that she can amass the money to bring them to Portland, where she had recently come to live.

In gratitude to Mr. Wescott, Mary Christmas bestows upon him and each member of his family the most valuable objects that she can excavate from the huge peddler's pack under whose weight she had walked the one hundred and fifty miles from Portland. The family treasure these offerings all their lives, but unknowingly Mary has given them much more priceless gifts. Most cherished among them is the gift of her own personality—a vital, wondrous force compounded of earthiness, love, duty, indomitability, and, above all, loyalty to family, friends, country, and the past. Contact with such a personality can have quick and lasting effects, particularly on children. As she listens to Mary Christmas and sees the traces of tears on her face, the oldest Wescott child, also named Mary, becomes aware dimly and fleetingly, at first, "that the sorrows in the world, the pitiful sufferings of the aged, the bewildering anguish of young people, the broken hearts of little children, are all a part of a great mantle of sorrow that encircles the whole wide earth in its dark, smothering folds. She drew back frightened . . . " (22). For the time she is spared further insight, but the following spring the experience is completed. A flowering crab-apple tree that in other Mays had thrilled her only with its beauty now hurt her with a pain sharper than any she had ever felt: "It had become lovely unto tears!" (42). When next she sees Mary Christmas, she perceives in her "what she never could have seen if the crab-apple tree had not finished what the traces of tears had begun" (49).

Cynthia, the younger Wescott girl, is not prone to feeling on quite so mystical a level, but her life too is redirected by the advent of this stranger from a far land. Under the spell of Mary Christmas and her wonderful stories of the saints, Cynthia discovers the power of words to convey beauty and to release the spirit. As did Miss Chase in the Montana ranges, she decides to devote her life to the creation and teaching of literature because she is passionately convinced that nothing is more worth doing.

These stories are Mary Christmas' gift to the children of the village; in their effect, they are second only to the vital presence of her character, from which indeed the stories are inseparable. The Wescott children, once they have heard them, pass them on to their playmates. One story is the legend of a pious bishop who went forth into the world carrying a silver box containing the hand of St. Gregory. With this relic he worked miracles of healing, not only of persons but of animals and plants, just as the mere story itself works miracles of transformation in the souls and imaginations of children like Cynthia, who herself would bring to the spiritually incomplete the medicine of great literature.

Another is the story of St. Jacob, who for three days struggled to climb Mt. Ararat where Noah's ark still rested and who, though he never reached the summit, was vouchsafed a plank from the ark. This plank, which was enshrined in a great church in Armenia, had cured Mary Christmas of an illness when, as a little girl, she had touched it. Miss Chase was always a critic of the starkness of the Congregationalism of her childhood. In her novel Mary Christmas' stories are a welcome corrective to this excessive bareness. Young imaginations crave such fare as necessary to their growth. To deny it to them is almost a cruelty.

Mary Christmas comes from an ancient land; she says it is the oldest in the world, for it was the site of the Garden of Eden. Bearing this past like her peddler's pack, she enters the clean, bright rawness of one of the newest lands on earth and from her inexhaustible stores of tradition and experience she gives unstintingly. If allegory is a hateful word, so be it; but there is allegory in this novel. America is a nation built on cultures brought from other lands. No one culture, like that of the English Puritans, can dare to exclude infusions of other traditions. It does so at its own risk—the risk of esthetic and spiritual malnutrition. The poorest immigrant from the poorest country may have contributions to make. Immediate and total Americanization of the newcomer is not to be desired. Not only can it cause family tragedy, as when Mary Christmas' son Raphael, brought to America with her hard-earned savings, adapts to his new environment by chewing gum, using slang, and speaking disrespectfully to his mother and refusing to talk to her in his native tongue; but it can result in a cultural loss to the nation. Mary Ellen Chase in *Mary Christmas* is making a plea for a more appreciative understanding of those whose hopes or misfortunes have brought them, strangers and alone, to a new country. The small-town fear of "foreigners," and the chauvinism of those who would Americanize at any cost, are not only inhumane but also short-sighted in their refusal to accept the cultural and spiritual riches the immigrants have to offer.

Of this little novel one can do no better than to paraphrase what Mary Ellen Chase, in *The Bible and The Common Reader*, wrote of the Book of Ruth, a favorite of hers, which she believes was written to counterbalance the ferocious clannishness of the Jews in the years following the Babylonian captivity, especially their abhorrence of mixed marriages. Though a foreigner, the Moabite Ruth makes a good and faithful wife. The story, Miss Chase writes, is without emotional profundity, is even sentimental and "sweet"—remarks which could also apply to *Mary Christmas*. Yet, Miss Chase continues, we should not expect the author of Ruth to transcend his own purpose, which was "to suggest by means of a lovely and idyllic story . . . that God is no respecter of persons, that human love is able to bridge the shallow differences of nationality, and that true religion is a matter of the heart and not of race."[4] This is precisely what *Mary Christmas,* a slight and at times sugary tale, suggests. If it does so effectively—and to many it undoubtedly does—it needs no other reason for being.

IV Uplands

Though the theme of *Mary Christmas* parallels that of Ruth, Miss Chase very likely did not have the scriptural story in mind as she wrote her novel. In her next novel, *Uplands,* which she published with Little, Brown in 1927, the Biblical influence is more direct, as it was to be in almost everything she wrote henceforth. The theme of *Uplands* is implicit in the phrase from Isaiah, "the shadow of a great rock in a weary land," which she quotes to describe the strength her heroine draws from the memories of her dead husband's love (151). The thought is of course the Dostoyevskian one already mentioned as being central in Miss Chase's outlook: we live on the resources of our memories, stored up from childhood. Good memories give us strength; they are "wells of living water," to use another of Miss Chase's favorite Biblical quotations (151).

In *Uplands* other influences are strong, especially that of Thomas Hardy. The setting is the coast of Eastern Maine, a region which Sarah Orne Jewett once described as a "Titanic sort of land." Here all the beauty, terror, and mystery of the ocean combine with the stern grandeur of a rocky hill country sweeping upward from the very shoreline. Enormous tides—ten or fourteen feet between high and low level—flow back and forth freshening creeks miles inland, flooding hill-bound coves where farmhouses crouch in loneliness, gurgling over mudflats and marshes, and crashing against the granite headlands. Here the spring is poignantly late, summer is brief and niggardly of warmth, and winter long and compassionless. Interminable fogs engulf land and sea in all seasons, but especially during the summer, chilling whatever warmth there is. Yet certain days in all months, particularly in September and October, bring dazzling calm and enchantment. The weather is a constant drama, galloping from climax to climax, now brightening, now darkening the lives of the coast dwellers.

The people of North Dorset, the fictional village of the novel, named after a part of the Hardy country, are the victims, the playthings, of the region and its climate, just as Hardy's people are puppets on the heaths and downs and moors of Wessex. Their joys and their sorrows are products of the land. Needless to say, the sorrows are more abundant than the joys, just as the soil yields cobblestones more bountifully than corn or potatoes. The horizons of the farm country are the sea and the hills. The villages are unimportant in the countrymen's lives—places where they go occasionally to church or to the shops—and the cities are totally beyond their ken. The people of *Uplands* are a generation removed from the farmer-fisherman, whose amphibious lives were bounded only by the limits of the ocean. Like the hulks of their fathers' boats rotting on the beaches, they are abandoned in disuse on tiny holdings never intended to yield a full livelihood. Deprived of the freedom of movement that the sea affords, they have become prisoners of an unfriendly land. Like Hardy's farmers and shepherds, their destinies are but pebbles in a stark geography. They have dwindled into pawns of climate, economics, and soil chemistry. Their struggles against natural forces have become feeble like those of the weaker animals. The epic battle of man against the elements no longer ennobles them. There is left only a grinding test of mere endurance, ending inevitably in listless resignation.

In depicting this environment Miss Chase is highly successful. She does not neglect its beauties, but in the context of the defeated lives of most of her characters the beauties become ironic mirages; only the grimness has substance. The tide, like the inexorable ebb and flow of the seasons, becomes a symbol of a destiny totally indifferent to human hopes and fears. The days of peace and beauty on the coast are pleasant deceptions. On such days, "one who did not know might well believe that the land was kind, that like the mountains of Israel, it would indeed bring peace to its people" (90). But such deceptions would be short-lived: "a cloud passed for a moment over the sun, and a great shadow stalked across the hills. From a beneficent land North Dorset grew in that instant black-browed, sullen, and menacing" (97). Even the illusory peace offered by the fair days is the "peace of resignation and acceptance, not of fulfillment and of plenty" (155). The momentary brightness cannot dispel the gloom from the mind of even a man in love.

> "I see the people here, and the land, and I get scared," [says Jarvis Craig, the hero, to his fiancée, Martha Crosby, who answers:] "We could never be like them, sweetheart. . . . We love each other too much. You're not afraid really, are you?"
>
> "I don't just know. Not while we're here together like this. But sometimes I get thinking. I suppose they never thought so either when they were young like us—folks, say, like my father and mother. And then by and by something caught them and shut them up, just as it caught me and shut me up till I'd known you" (95-96).

The Hardy motif, so far as life in North Dorset goes, is unalloyed. Jarvis Craig, the son of a farming couple whose lives have turned to stone, falls in love with a servant girl, Martha, whose old-maid mistress finds the only outlet for her frustration in distributing Bibles and converting souls even more frustrated than herself. The farm boy and hired girl have their brief May-time idyll of love, get secretly married in a nearby county town (an American Casterbridge), and a few weeks later Jarvis, instantly killed by an overturning haywagon, is laid to rest in the family burial plot back of the Craig barn. Martha, devastated, but unable to bring herself to reveal her marriage, escapes to a distant convent, escorted by Colin Holliday, an aspirant to the priesthood and son of a North Dorset man who had shocked the village by leaving the coast and marrying an Irish Catholic girl. Miss Chase's description of the convent echoes her own happy times at St. Catherine's. Under the care of the sisters, the Protestant Martha is soothed by a "sense of safety and of quietness," by a "consciousness of order and simplicity" (222). But a spell of sickness proves to be the result of pregnancy, and she finally tells the nuns of her marriage. She returns to the Craig farm, which for the first time in years becomes a place of hope and human warmth. Martha is now indeed under the shadow of a great rock in a weary land. Even after the death of her husband the fact of their love shelters her from the spiritual drying up which is the lot of most of the inhabitants of North Dorset:

> She needed no metaphysician or mystic to tell her that the only real tragedy is the lack of that abundant life which in its spiritual fullness can triumph over all the sad variety of earthly pain. That lack, she knew, was the tragedy she had feared and fled from. The isolation and poverty of North Dorset, the losing fight against a barren land, these were in themselves but its able handmaidens and henchmen; reticence and restraint the chains they forged and bound with. Sarah Craig [Jarvis' mother] had known that tragedy and had been unable to keep open her way out; she and Jarvis through their new love had escaped it . . . (278).

When Martha Crosby dies in childbirth, one does not have the feeling that she has lived futilely. Thus toward the end, the novel abandons the determinism that is evident in the first two thirds of it. The chains of forty years of failure fall even from Ethan and Sarah Craig as they take their orphaned grandchild into their hearts. Jude the Obscure in the fullness of defeat could quote only Job's curse upon the day he was born, but Sarah recalls "from somewhere, far back in almost forgotten years," the comforting words of Isaiah: "He hath sent me to bind up the brokenhearted, to proclaim liberty to the captives, and the opening of the prisons to them that are bound. . . . To give unto them beauty for ashes, the oil of joy for mourning, the garment of praise for the spirit of heaviness" (293).

The old countrywoman's grasping the baby as her deliverer and her memory of the Old Testament words that were supposed to foretell the coming of the Saviour are believable, even convincing. But the same scene, that immediately following Martha's death, is flawed by the unexpected appearance of two persons, apparently Colin Holliday and a priest, who utter Latin words over Sarah's corpse: "Requiem aeternan dona eae, Domine, et lux perpetua luceat eae" (292). The Naturalistic grimness of the setting has been too effectively conveyed for even the mighty syllables of Isaiah and the Requiem to annul it totally. It is difficult to credit these sudden floods of light on both the living and the dead. We have seen in Sarah or in her husband no signs of a faith, either dormant or active, that could be so instantaneously resurrected either by the boy or by the Latin and English messages of hope and peace.

Miss Chase, however, carefully indicates in the motto of the novel—a passage "adapted from an Old Play"—that the book is neither tragedy nor comedy, but romance. Seemingly she did not intend the Hardy effects to extend much beyond her presentation of environment as a strongly determining but not totally inexorable influence upon the persons unfortunate enough to live in it. She parts company with Hardy in permitting some of her people to triumph over their surroundings. The element of romance is further enhanced by the presence of Colin Holliday, the would-be priest. His elfin flittings through the book; his quoting from Irish fairy tales, which Martha learns to love; his depositing of sonnets in the hollows of old trees for Martha to pick up—strike a false note which does much to spoil the plot even of a romance.

Uplands is apparently no longer read. It is the weakest of Miss Chase's books for adults, weaker certainly than the lighthearted *Mary Christmas.* Yet it has its strong points—vivid descriptions of nature, the evocation of haunting atmosphere and mood, and stretches of powerful narration. The handling of Jarvis' death, and its shock as sudden in the book as an accident in real life, and the account of the funeral and its aftermath completely command the reader's emotions. The convent scenes, taken by themselves, are interesting and humorous. At least one character—oddly, the least likable in the book—is skillfully drawn. This is Abby Wickham, Martha's sour-tempered mistress, who finds her own salvation in saving the souls of others in the remoter hamlets of the Maine coast and who consummates her life in marriage with a fellow evangelist. The asperity of her religion contrasts most unfavorably with the humanity and humor of the nuns to whom Martha flees.

Uplands in actuality is an expansion of a short story, "The Garment of Praise," which Mary Ellen Chase had published two years earlier (October, 1925) in *Scribner's.* This story, which takes the title from the psalm that Sarah Craig quotes in both the long and short narratives, has the same characters; but Martha's last name and her mistress' whole name are changed in the later version. The short story begins on the day of Jarvis' funeral—Jarvis was killed, as in the book, under a load of hay—and carries on through Martha's death in childbirth and

Sarah's spiritual rebirth in the advent of a grandchild. Colin Holliday is totally absent, as are the convent scenes and the Roman Catholic motif—in other words, most of what makes the novel a romance rather than realistic fiction. One scene, that of the thunderstorm after Jarvis' burial, is almost the same in both story and novel, even in the phrasing; but it is more impressive in the story because it occupies proportionately more space.

To Sarah the storm is a comfort. Though she cannot express her own emotions—years of merciless holding herself in have made that impossible—yet in the discharge of lightning and the wild sweep of wind and rain she can vicariously experience relief. Also, the storm provides a subject of conversation with her husband Ethan. When Martha, less repressed because younger, does throw herself on the table in despair, Sarah envies her. And when she further gives vent to her feelings by moving to Jarvis' old place at the table, the climax of both story and novel is reached. In retaining this scene, Miss Chase gave her book its most dramatic moments.

But one change in the novel is difficult to explain. In "The Garment of Praise" Martha is not wedded to Jarvis; the child is illegitimate and the grandmother's emotions after its birth are more chaotic and conflicting. Yet love overrides her Calvinistic abhorrence of the situation, and she learns of one of life's paradoxes: out of sin can come joy, out of evil good. But in *Uplands,* where Jarvis and Martha have been properly married, Sarah is spared any such jolts and adjustments of her feelings.

In her book on Thomas Hardy, Miss Chase condemns the magazine publishers for forcing Hardy to render innocuous his scenes that dealt frankly and realistically with sexual irregularities, as his readers might view them. Nor does Miss Chase completely exonerate Hardy for permitting such violence to be done his art. Yet in *Uplands* she has bowdlerized her own art. It is not a question of realism—it is equally possible that the couple be married or unmarried. But the inner conflict and tension of the characters—Martha's anguish over Jarvis' death, and Sarah's confusion in the final scene—are materially lessened by the change. Considering Miss Chase's purpose of making *Uplands* a romance, the change may have been justifiable. But the grimness of setting of most of the book—the bleak Craig household and the prison-like atmosphere of Abby Wickham's farm—lend themselves to the situations of "The Garment of Praise" rather than to the fantasy and whimsicality of *Uplands.* The same basic plot has made a strong short story and a weak novel.

V *Miss Chase's Manner of Writing*

Though teaching continued throughout her life to hold her first allegiance, with the publication of two novels Miss Chase was far within the promised land of authorship. Already in her textbooks she had formulated certain definite ideas about narrative, fiction, and the essay. As authorship became more and more a part of her life, she fell into certain practices—she herself would reject the term *methods* as too grandiose—in her daily stints of composition. These practices, and the attitudes that prompted them, deserve consideration in the examination of her writing. How an author works is undoubtedly never of prime importance, but it is of some significance and always of interest.

Miss Chase's creative procedures involve nothing so sensational as Thomas Wolfe's ledgers bulging with purple prose or Sinclair Lewis' months of research and his lengthy preparatory biographies of all his characters. Miss Chase regards a book as a job to be done as well as she can do it, not unlike the preparation of a meal or the planning of a class hour. She lives mentally with a book for months or years before she starts putting it on paper. By that time it has taken such definite form that she needs no written outline except perhaps a list of chapters. She does most of her writing in the morning at the rate of one to two thousand words a day. She composes in pencil in copybooks, carefully formulating her sentences in her mind and occasionally repeating them aloud to herself, sometimes while walking about the house, until they sound right to her. Only when fully satisfied does she commit a sentence to writing.

Consequently, revision plays a small part in Miss Chase's work. She rarely makes false starts. When she copies her manuscripts for her typists, again in pencil, she may alter a word now and then or rewrite a sentence. But, on the whole, her second copies are merely more legible versions of the originals.

Much of Miss Chase's writing has been done at Smith, where her schedule was arranged to give her several days a week free from classes. She has also written during her stays in England, notably at Grantchester in Cambridgeshire in 1935 and 1936. She is, however, an author who can utilize any tag end of time that makes itself available, and she has little sympathy for students who demand perfect conditions for study. She herself has done much writing on railroad trains and during waits at God-forsaken junctions between trains. But much of her finest work was done at "Windswept," her summer home at Petit Manan Point, Maine, for sixteen years, though her early morning walks, gardening, and flounder fishing cut into her time there. At "Windswept" there remained something of the pristine quality of the coast—some of the sweep and grandeur of shore and sky and sea that had been there before Champlain and the early settlers. Best of all, perhaps, the tourists thronged less numerously so far east, and the summer cottagers were fewer. This corner of Maine still belonged to the fishermen, the farmers, the blueberry pickers on the burnt-over barrens that rolled back from the sea.

CHAPTER 4

The Maine Novels

THOUGH *Uplands* and *Mary Christmas* had been favorably reviewed, Mary Ellen Chase produced no fiction between 1927 and 1934 except several short stories and a book for children, *The Silver Shell.* But it was not a period of idleness; during it she published a book of essays; a textbook for freshman English courses, that went through two subsequent editions; and her masterpiece of non-fiction, *A Goodly Heritage.* In 1934 appeared *Mary Peters,* her third novel for adults and one of her best. *Mary Peters* is among the three books, *Silas Crockett* and *The Edge of Darkness* being the other two, that Miss Chase calls her "Maine novels."

I *Rusticators and Natives*

Mary Peters is a monument to the Maine seafaring women, now as extinct as the sailing ships that once carried them around the world. Miss Chase celebrates the historical period in which flowered this finest type of New England womanhood by contrasting the fullness of the past with the sterility and emptiness of the present, a contrast made by Sarah Orne Jewett sixty years earlier in *Deephaven,* a volume of sketches of a once-prosperous seaport whose commerce had vanished and whose harbor had filled with silt. In her Preface to *Deephaven* Sarah Orne Jewett stated that one of her purposes in writing the book was to make known to summer visitors the real qualities of the coastal people who were often regarded as bumpkins or tramps by sojourners from the city. In other words, she was on the defensive; she was indignant at the lack of respect on the part of outsiders toward her own people. This same motif, intensified, may be found in *Mary Peters,* in which the slow but irreversible encroachment of "summer people" on the territory and lives of the old residents of the coast is an important theme and a source of conflict.

To Sarah Orne Jewett and to Miss Chase, the summer people's almost studied ignorance of the history and the cultural significance of the places they were overrunning amounted to a rejection of tradition itself, and to both these Maine women tradition is synonymous with civilization. Disregard of tradition is a symptom of a new barbarism menacing the country.

The antagonism between the summer vacationers and the all-year inhabitants is a social phenomenon peculiar perhaps to America and especially to New England. It may seem trivial both from the literary and the sociological points of view, but it is a blemish and an inconsistency in American democracy, though one which at present shows signs of disappearing. In *Mary Peters* Miss Chase describes what occurred from the Civil War onward in all the mountain and seashore resorts of New England. Wealthy families from the large cities purchased or built houses in the older rural and coastal communities, where they would spend the summer months living in a style completely beyond the reach of the local residents. There were, of course, no differences in race or religion, or even in cultural heritage. On the whole the two groups, at least in the beginning, were of Yankee stock, were Protestant, and held to the same social and political ideals. Nor was there an unbridgeable gulf in education. The country academies, as we have seen, were excellent; in fact, some of them, like Exeter and Andover, had become nationally known and were attended by the children of the urban élite, as was the case with originally rural colleges like Amherst, Bowdoin, and Dartmouth.

Furthermore, the city folk, if they cared to, could trace their ancestry back to the same kind of village that they were now returning to for their summerings. Henry Ward Beecher's statement about the village being the brood comb of New England excellence must be borne in mind. It was a rare village indeed that did not contribute a famous editor, publisher, educator, clergyman, or industrialist to the national life. Through these men, the village had set the standards and the values of the nation. Yet the descendants of the same country people who brought the village qualities to the cities either ignored, or condescended to, their own stock during summer vacations. The villagers, of course, were resentful, and a wide and almost unpassable rift resulted. Marriages between country and city persons were virtually unheard of and, to most, unthinkable. Social mingling seldom occurred; and, if it did at some public function like a church supper, it was stiff and self-conscious. "Natives" sold their heirlooms and their ancient family mansions to the newcomers and hated themselves for succumbing—and the city people for tempting them.

This division, which can be attributed to no deep-rooted cultural difference, must have been the result of rivalry or competitiveness, which in itself is a basic characteristic of American life, rural or urban. Worldly success has always ranked high in the so-called Protestant ethic. The man who flourishes in his calling, whether it be farming, business, or preaching, must be favored by the Lord and therefore may safely be assumed to be of the elect. By the late nineteenth century, any such theological view of material prosperity may have become only a rather strong vestigial element in the thinking of most Americans. But the notion that the best people are those who make the most money or sway the most power was also being propagated by the Darwinian philosophies, especially in the work of the extremely popular Herbert Spencer.

The city dweller, returning for the summer to the countryside that his forebears had deserted a generation or so earlier, would naturally feel superior to even the best educated countryman. A carriage and a coachman, a staff of house servants, well-tailored clothes of costly fabrics, a more complex etiquette, a background of European travel, even a different, though somewhat colorless, way of speaking the mother tongue—all tended to elevate him in his own opinion above the rural dweller whose cool climate and pleasant scenery he had come temporarily to enjoy. Deep within him the countryman would have to concur with this estimate; the newcomer must be better, for look how well he lives, how much money he spends, what influence he wields. In a feudal society such an admission would not lead to bad feeling; some people are born to a higher station than others, and we must look up to and, if possible, love our betters, who in turn are obliged to love us. But in a society where, politically at least, all are supposed to be equal, it takes more than Calvin or Darwin to reconcile a man to the idea that another, no matter how impressive his manner of living and his bank account, has a right to act as if he were superior. The pill is too bitter to swallow without protesting gags and grimaces. Thus estrangement, contempt, and finally spite combine to divide fellow citizens, notwithstanding the closest ties of blood and culture.

II Mary Peters: *Acceptance but Not Resignation*

Mary Peters covers the period in which much of the Maine coast switched from seafaring and fishing to catering to the "rusticators"—the decades from 1880 to 1920. Like Sarah Peters, the mother of Mary, Miss Chase cherishes the maritime past of Maine. To them both there is "something immeasurably sad... in the sight of a grandson of a shipmaster in the foreign trade shingling the roof of a summer cottage for his livelihood... something sadder in the knowledge that the strangers, who by their demands supplied that livelihood, knew little and cared less for the boy's history" (185). And, like Sarah Peters, Mary Ellen Chase, who grew up in the same period as that covered by the novel, saw that the wall between "sojourners and natives" was yearly increasing in height and thickness.

And, again like Sarah Peters, who had spent most of her adult life on ships sailing to the most distant parts of the world, Mary Ellen Chase after years of travel and college teaching could judge Maine character with objectivity. In it she saw weaknesses which would lay it open to temptations presented by moneyed outsiders—temptations to discard dignity and even integrity and honor for ready cash, to play the role of a servant rather than of a freeman farmer or a fisherman. The weakness was an excessive shrewdness, developed through generations of struggle with a hostile environment ashore and at sea, which "under the mellowing influences of contact with other lands and other minds... lost itself in a humourous kind of wisdom," but which "under more narrowing influences... doubled back upon itself, became more acute, subtle, cunning even" (301). Thus fishermen discarded their lines and nets to conduct vacationing bankers on picnics; merchants raised their prices beyond enough to ensure a fair profit. Young people, students in the excellent old academies, gave up their plans for college to become the maids and gardeners of the rich.

The greed and servility of the "natives" lowered them in the estimation of those who hired them. Having the souls of lackeys, these people should be treated like lackeys. The villagers began to dream of living lives like their masters'. Foolish girls and their ambitious mothers yearned for marriages, which seldom occurred, with the sons of the wealthy cottagers. Boys would futilely eye the lovely, haughty daughters of the rich and dream of never-to-be romances. Dreams of wealth and ease replaced those of high adventure in far-off seas, and the dreams inevitably paved the way to bitterness and frustration. An unhappier, quicker transformation of a once proud and independent people would be hard to find.

Yet the decline was not complete, nor did it, even in a lesser degree, engulf everbody. While admitting that the Maine character has weaknesses, Mary Ellen Chase has never lost faith in it nor in American character in general, of which that of New England is prototypal. The capitulation to easy money on the Maine coast represents a nationwide tendency, a cheapening of values, a coarsening of ambitions, a loss of collective and individual integrity. "A quick buck" from the summer folks is no different from a quick buck from the stock exchange, unscrupulous advertising, or an inflated real-estate market. When money is valued more highly than character, and ease than useful labor, a society is in a bad way. Miss Chase makes all this clear in her novels, but she knows also that there are certain depths and strengths in the human spirit which even the most tawdry times cannot completely neutralize.

In Mary Peters, as well as in her brother and parents, these strengths are a bastion against anything that life may bring. The book ends with Mary's discovery that her years have come in a perfect circle from the bliss of a childhood awakening to beauty to the bliss of a mature realization that life is "a kind of waiting—a waiting upon the graciousness and bounty of the things which had been, in order that the things to come might find one free and unafraid" (377). It is for the motto of *Mary Peters* that Miss Chase quotes Alyosha Karamazov's thought that illuminates so much of her writing: good childhood memories are indispensable to a good life.

Mary Peters, like Miss Chase herself, cherishes an armory of such memories from her childhood spent on her father's ship sailing from port to port around the world. Most dazzling among them is the memory of Cadiz shining on the shores of Spain. The white city of Cadiz awakened her soul. It was a symbolic city, symbolizing Mary never quite knew what. But its image was imprinted in the core of her consciousness—an image of beauty, purity, and freedom from the frigid chains of New England restraint—all that is best and most lasting in life and which brings life closest to immortality and eternity. At the end of the book, when her life has completed its circle, she reproduces the image of the city, which she had seen only once at the age of nine, in a hooked rug made with such skill that it elevates rug hooking, by which Mary is now earning her living, to the level of a fine art. This masterpiece she will not sell, despite the urgings and exclamations of delight of the summer people who have been eager customers for her less treasured rugs.

Most poignant among Mary Peters' memories is that of Mr. Gardiner, one of her father's officers. It was Mr. Gardiner, a former schoolmaster, who first opened to Mary at the age of fourteen, the pages of great books—Catullus and Shakespeare—and whom Mary loved as she would never again love anyone. He revealed to her her capacity to love, and this capacity, realized along with her awareness of beauty, carries her through the worst trials of her life, even spiritualizing her marriage with Jim Pendleton, a union that to most would have been unmitigated horror.

Jim Pendleton is the son of a French woman and a Maine sea captain who had once been in love with Mary Peters' mother Sarah. The marriage with the French woman had been one not of love but of necessity. Jim, whose physical lameness suggests his flawed character, is a moody, unhappy, but musically talented boy. Coming from France to Petersport, Maine, to attend its academy, he lives aloof, a misfit with his foreign appearance and manner. But Sarah Peters, who would have married his father had things been otherwise, befriends Jim, treating him as a son; and he in his loneliness responds to her mothering. Later he has an affair with Hester, Mary's best friend. Then, suddenly giving up his plans for college, he goes to New York to try to live by his music. Hester, who has become pregnant by him, dies in childbirth. Even then Sarah protects Jim, especially against her son John, who had hoped to marry Hester.

Years later, after the death of Sarah, Mary marries Jim; and for a time he earns his living selling phonographs to the farmers and fishermen along the coast. But eventually he lapses into dependency on Mary, who has taken a job schoolteaching. Mary is wise enough to understand that he will not, and cannot, be faithful to her or to any other woman. When his moodiness becomes intense, she encourages him to make long visits to New York, knowing, of course the dissipation and infidelity he will fall into there. Even in Petersport he has been having an affair with a schoolmate of Mary's, Ellen Kimball, the young widow of Mary's brother John. The evening that Jim is to leave for France, his mother's homeland, to join a volunteer ambulance corps in World War I, he drives with Ellen to a distant town and on the way home is killed in an automobile crash that leaves Ellen a lifelong cripple. But, in spite of his spending his last night in America with another woman, Mary retains a loving memory of him. And far from hating Ellen, she nurses her throughout her querulous cripple's life at John's old farm when poverty forces them to retire from the town. The love released so many years before by Mr. Gardiner is selfless enough to rise above jealousy and to ignore affront.

In the last scene in the novel Mr. Gardiner returns to Mary in vivid memory when his nephew, also named Gardiner, a summer resident, calls to inquire about his uncle, who had sailed with a man named Peters from this town. More sympathetic and sensitive than most of the summer people, he expresses regret at the change that has come over the coast, and he ends his conversation by saying to Mary: "You seem to know the things that all people ought to know, but don't" (374). What she knows comes not so much from books, though Mary Ellen Chase is the last to downgrade this type of learning, but from life—from her mother and from Mr. Gardiner, from the earth, "the ancient life-giver," and from the "broad-backed sea," which is "the dispenser of many gifts" (377).

The earth and the sea are indeed the ultimate forces in the lives of the Peters women, who are the morally strong characters in the novel. In both Mary, who had been born aboard ship in the harbor of Singapore, and in her mother "the sea had wrought its steady, intangible nourishment, the power and security of which only later years on the land would reveal" (33).

But Mary's brother John, though he spends his early years at sea, is by nature a son of the soil. In his later boyhood he is left at home to work on his uncle's farm, which he finally comes to own and which he lives on and cultivates till his death beneath a falling limb. Animals, the changing seasons, the sprouting and maturing crops, above all the continuity of life on the land are the stays of John's spirit. "It was perhaps the remnant of that Saxon heritage . . . which still fills one's heart at the sight of his own roof-slopes and lighted windows beneath them, making one still aware in the midst of a hurrying and changing world of the long, patient ritual of home" (265). Both the seafaring and the farming life are based on tradition, which to Mary Ellen Chase is inseparable from a meaningful existence. Thus, when John's wife Ellen, an insensitive nagger, fails him, he falls back on the soil, which cannot fail him, for it is "the source of his spirit" (233).

Since the earth and the sea are the mainsprings of life and its values in *Mary Peters,* the novel is rich in descriptions of ocean and farm and of the coastal village of Petersport, which divides its existence between the land and the water. Daily living on shipboard is unfolded before our eyes in all its detail—the weeks in the doldrums, the cracking monsoons, the schooling of the captain's children, the death of pet dogs and cats on board, the near mutinies, the interludes on land at Cadiz or Singapore. Miss Chase's own countless childhood hours of reliving with her grandmother and other former seafarers, men and women, their experiences aboard ship and in foreign ports are responsible for the vividness of this writing. No research in libraries could ever produce these pages. They are transcriptions of living narratives that were ingrained in the listener from her earliest years.

Farming was even closer to Miss Chase's experience, since she had lived essentially a country life but had never been to sea on a sailing merchantman. More than any of her other books *Mary Peters* is redolent of the sights, colors, sounds, smells, and dialect of the Maine farm. Nothing escapes her.

Here is the change of the seasons: "Woodlots flamed in October, were still in November, received in December their snows and in March the clinging mists which at once hid and nurtured their springing life. Fields held the mellow October sunlight, changing beneath it to the warm tans of Indian summer.

Oaks purpled the distant hillsides, their more tenacious leaves fading slowly into the russet hues of early winter, paling before the first snows" (220).

Or the odors of the one-room rural school where Mary taught for a while:

> When she bent over the boys at their desks on spring mornings, she smelled barn smells, fresh milk, hayseed, manure, mingled with the scent of pine pitch which lingered on their fingers from the pricking of pine blisters and with that of the wood which they had carried into their mothers' wood-boxes on their morning chores. . . . There were smells of soda-biscuits, flapjacks and doughnuts. Breakfasts were thus easily discerned. There were smells of lampwicks and soft soap, homemade sausage and apple butter, smells of wood smoke, horse liniments, spruce gum, ham, and baked potatoes, apples, baked beans and johnny-cake and buttered popcorn. Colds brought more smells and made one keenly aware of the rigours of rural pharmacopaeia. Flannel chest protectors gave infallible proof of the plasters and poultices they had replaced, plasters of mustard and salt pork, hen's oil and duck's grease, boiled onions and flaxseed. Homemade cough syrup lingered in the warm close air . . . (222-23).

Or rural saws and maxims, particularly from the weather-lore that connects the countryman so closely to the elements in which he works and lives: "A snowy February . . . promised a fine summer. Thunder in March was a bad sign for harvest. Stone walls piled in October on the three days of the hunters' moon assured a farmer of the friendliness of his neighbors for a full year at least. One should never speak of secret matters in a field full of little hills when the moon was waning" (218).

The lives of sailors and farmers are deeply enfolded in tradition, and yet, as Miss Chase depicts them, they are always subject to accident. In all her books fate, or luck, plays a prominent part in shaping her characters' destinies, but in none so much as in *Mary Peters.* Fate deals five major or unexpected blows: the shipwreck in which Mary's father and Mr. Gardiner are drowned, and which sends the family permanently back to Maine; Hester's death in childbirth, which blights John's hopes and which darkens the lives of Sarah, Mary, and Jim, who is responsible for her pregnancy; John's death beneath a tree limb, which releases Ellen to do violence to Jim's and Mary's marriage;

Sarah's stroke, which results not in tragedy but in the further spiritualizing of her life; and the motor accident, which kills Jim and makes Ellen a permanent invalid.

This question arises: Are these misfortunes simply *dei ex machina*? To Mary Ellen Chase they are not, any more than the accidents in Thomas Hardy's novels are to him. The unavoidable and the unexpected are part of life; farming and sailing are dangerous occupations; automobile accidents kill tens of thousands every year; old ladies are prone to strokes; and young ones are prone to getting pregnant in or out of wedlock. Over such occurrences humanity has no foolproof control. They must be met with acceptance but not with resignation. For, if man cannot avoid the bludgeonings of fate, he can yet survive them with dignity if he draws strength from the deepest sources of his being—the sources of love and compassion. Thus Sarah Peters, paralyzed by a stroke, forgets her own plight and ceases even to worry about the inevitable misery that she sees slowly engulfing the marriage of John and Ellen. In place of worry had come a pity for "a certain necessary sorrow and desolation in the circumstance of human existence, in the very manner by which men through some mischance had from the beginning lived their lives. She felt this pity for John and Ellen, for herself, for all other souls throughout the world. Since things were so, she thought, this sense of universal sympathy, this compassion for humanity, created of itself a certainty, a faith, without which men and women could not live, unconscious though they might be of its hourly alleviation" (282). Much the same kind of strength carries Mary through her ordeal with Jim and later leads her to care for crippled Ellen. John, when his marriage crumbles, gains strength from immersion in the cycle of life and growth of which he is a part as a farmer. In the case of all three, there is acceptance but not resignation or defeat.

In this novel is revealed much of Mary Ellen Chase's religious thought. She is impatient, of course, with the two brands of narrowness purveyed by the Petersport Congregational and Methodist churches. Their emphasis on sin, retribution, and the like make her shudder. The yearly revivals, sponsored by both churches, disgust her. Salvation comes not by way of an emotional orgy, induced by hysterical preaching, but, as Sarah explains to Mary, "at odd moments when you're not expecting it. . . . by thoughts you have that are sent to you every now and then. . . . by people you care for. (Mary thought of Mr. Gardiner and then of Hester.) And sometimes just by things you see like some of the things we used to see when we sailed—things we weren't expecting. (Mary thought of Cadiz and light flooded her face once more)" (168). The religious experience occurs in flashes of recognition of the eternal in the temporal, "rare moments which came and went, which could not be sought or asked for, but by which one steered one's course, wholly alive only while they lasted" (33). Thus, as Dostoyevsky's Father Zossima says, we live in paradise all our lives if only we have eyes to see it. Sarah does see it, at certain moments all her life, but continuously after her illness. Mary at the end comes to understand that Earth reveals "in summer secrets magical enough to give to men and women who [live] upon it the life of the Immortals" (361).

In an article entitled "My Novels about Maine," Miss Chase has much to say about *Mary Peters*—its genesis, its writing, and her feelings about it. The novel had been germinating in her mind, she writes, for at least twenty-five years. She entirely agrees with Sarah Orne Jewett's statement to Willa Cather that a book that has had a long life in the writer's thoughts and imagination will be a better book when finally put on paper than if written without delay. The seed of *Mary Peters* was the stories told Miss Chase as a girl by her grandmother. The grandmother's life, like Sarah Peters', had been dominated by the vision of Cadiz, where she had sometimes stayed while her husband traded up and down the Mediterranean. Without the symbol of Cadiz, the book would have been a very different and inferior one. Indeed, it has become a symbol in Mary Ellen Chase's life as well. It appears over and over again in her novels, children's stories, and essays. She herself treasures an ancient map of the city and harbor, supposedly the site of the Biblical Tarshish and in Roman times a place known for its gaiety and good living. But in all her travels she has never visited Cadiz, for she has "learned that symbols do not often bear exploration."[1]

Mary Ellen Chase owes to her grandmother much more than images and episodes and even the remarkable symbol of Cadiz. The ultimate excellence of Miss Chase's sea novels, not only *Mary Peters,* is the feeling about the sea, the profound understanding of its effect on human beings, that underlies all the plots and descriptions. "My grandmother," she writes, "always hated and feared the sea. . . . Yet she understood what it had to give to women of her generation who loved their shipmaster husbands *too* much to remain at home while they sailed upon it. And this perception she somehow managed to convey to me as a child—this understanding of its gifts as well as of its terrors, this sense of a great and various world beyond our own small harbor and our own Maine hills."[2]

Other details for *Mary Peters* came from her student days at the University of Maine, where she met the children of a famous Maine shipping family—the Colcords of Searsport, who had been prepared for college while at sea, their mother and ship's officers, like Mr. Gardiner, being their teachers. During Miss Chase's numerous crossings of the Atlantic, she spent as much time as possible on deck taking notes on the appearance and behavior of the ocean, the weather, and the birds.

Miss Chase believes "that no character in pure fiction is *ever* founded upon any actual person."[3] Though mannerisms, peculiarities of speech, appearance, or dress observed in real people may go into the making of a character, he still belongs only in the imaginary world of the author. Sarah Peters is in some ways suggestive of Miss Chase's grandmother, but she is not a life portrait. Mary Peters, whose name is that of Miss Chase's great-great-grandmother, is more an idea than a person. "She was created solely for the purpose of showing how a childhood spent largely at sea might help to form a mind and an imagination invulnerable against time, chance, and tragedy."[4]

III Silas Crockett

Mary Ellen Chase has written that the "inheritance of imperishable values" that is her birthright as a daughter of one of the Maine seafaring families has imposed upon her "a debt which cannot possibly either be underestimated or ever fully discharged."[5] In her novels about Maine, however, she has made the attempt to pay the debt; and in none, she feels, has she come closer to success than in *Silas Crockett*. She wrote this second novel while on leave from Smith during 1934 and 1935 and in the English village of Grantchester within sight of Cambridge across the East Anglian meadows. Never had she more congenial surroundings for writing, nor fewer distractions. Her cheery living-room fire, the bleating of lambs in nearby folds, the efficiency of her English housekeeper freed her mind and spirit for the most ambitious literary task she had yet undertaken.

Silas Crockett (1935) is historical fiction. Her most carefully documented novel, she considers it her most valuable contribution to the understanding of her native state. In it she dramatizes one hundred years of the maritime history of Maine and, by extension, of New England and all America. Dedicated "to the seafaring families of Maine and to their descendants, who still retain within themselves the graciousness and the dignity of their heritage," it covers the years 1830-1933, or four generations, of the annals of such a family, the Crocketts. The setting is Saturday Cove, just east of Mt. Desert, a section of coast that Miss Chase especially loves, perhaps because it has been less ravaged by "the summer industry" than has her own Blue Hill Bay. The town, though fictional, is typical in its one-hundred-and-fifty-year-old existence as a port.

In her Foreword, Miss Chase acknowledges her indebtedness to various historical works, among them Samuel Eliot Morison's *The Maritime History of Massachusetts,* Arthur H. Clark's *The Clipper Ship Era,* and Raymond Macfarlane's *A History of New England Fisheries*—all definitive works about their subjects. Some of her material, such as that on Maine meeting houses, came from her Maine coast friends. Vast amounts, the core of the novel, came from her own experience and observation.

Some novels are not only works of literature but lasting source books of social history. *Silas Crockett* is one of them, even more than *Mary Peters.* Scarcely a custom or folkway, not a sound, smell, or sight important or trivial, that could be observed in Saturday Cove during the one hundred years of the novel's coverage is omitted. One hears the mallets and saws, smells the tar and hemp of the shipyards, sees the sleek vessels slide down the ways in the great shipping decade of the 1830's, and walks the streets with the outlandish sailors just off ships from Rio or Cadiz. Later one scents the mackerel and herring shoveled by scale-flecked fishermen from holds of schooners in from the Banks during the less glamorous years when Saturday Cove lived by fishing. One attends weddings, births, funerals, and bubble-blowing parties with the children, sharing the joy and sorrow of each.

Of course, as always in Mary Ellen Chase's books, the seasons, the landscape, the changing face of the sea are described with an accuracy and a poetry that only one who has lived on the Maine coast is capable of admiring sufficiently. The town characters—the schoolmaster, the Calvinist parson, the town crier—are typical, as well as convincing, individuals. The major characters, the Crocketts and their womenfolk, are, Miss Chase says, typical of people she has known all her life; but they are not based on actual persons, dead or alive.

The history of Saturday Cove falls into several periods, each marking a decline from the previous one. The book opens at the beginning of the clipper-ship era; but on the first page is planted the virus of decay. Silas Crockett is presented to us as he returns to Saturday Cove by coastal steamboat from Boston, where he has just terminated one of his Far Eastern voyages. The steamer, a grimy, wallowing hulk, captained by a seaman of second-rate abilities, is the harbinger of the age of steam that spelled the doom of the clippers even before they had been designed or built.

Silas is the son of James and Abigail Crockett. James had been a privateer in the Revolutionary War and had later traded back and forth around the world, fighting with pirates and prospering commercially. He had owned the shipyards at Saturday Cove and occupied one of its most stately houses, which had been given him as a wedding gift in 1798 by his father Amos, also a sea captain and one of the founders of Saturday Cove. Silas' mother, the former Abigail Shaw, herself the daughter of a wealthy and daring seafaring family of Salem, had spent much of her life waiting for various relatives to return from their voyages—first her father and brothers, then her husband and sons. Some of them never returned: her brother Nathan was killed in a fight with the Malays; her oldest son Nicholas succumbed to fever at the age of nineteen off West Africa; and her second son, Reuben, went down with his ship, no one knew where.

When Silas returns in 1830 to Saturday Cove it is at the high-water mark of its and New England's maritime ascendency, and therefore of the Crockett family's power and wealth. The year also marks a high point in Silas' personal life, for he has returned to marry Solace Winship. Solace is the daughter of an architect, Thomas Winship, who during his life designed fourteen meeting houses, eighty-four dwelling houses, eighty-three vessels, and twelve schoolhouses. The marriage is almost an allegory. For, if men like the impetuous, far-voyaging, amazingly vital Crocketts are responsible for the material wealth of the coast—the shipyards and the commerce—men like Thomas Winship, with a meditative and artistic bent, bring to its villages a beauty that persists generations after the glory of the old merchant-adventurers has crumbled into dust.

The New England port towns, especially those of Maine, have few rivals anywhere in the world for their simple, impressive dignity. Thomas Winship is typical of the men responsible for them. For twenty years a ship's carpenter, he had observed and absorbed the architectural styles of many civilizations. An artist as well as a craftsman, he finally left the sea to work on land. "Into his work he . . . wrought details of the buildings he had seen throughout the world, Greek temples, English cathedrals, Georgian mansions, Roman columns and porticoes" (29). His masterpieces were his churches, and among the best of them was the one which he constructed at Saturday Cove, for it "bore evidence of an assimilation common to a hundred other rural builders along the coast of Maine. . . . For the New England meeting-house in its best and noblest form is an incorporation, a unification, a synthesis of the art and the architecture of many centuries, many lands, and many peoples" (29).

America itself, Miss Chase would seem to say, is such a synthesis; and, when that synthesis flowers as it did on the New England coast in the 1830's, American civilization is at its best. But not only is the blending one of forms and styles; it is also one of esthetic sensibility with the Puritan qualities of commercial shrewdness, pride in work, courage, and rigid moral standards, without all of which there would have been neither the money, the skill, nor the persistence to build the towns themselves. The New England ports are monuments to the Puritan way of life, as well as to the synthesizing proclivity of American culture.

Silas' life is one of almost complete fulfillment. Though the steamboat becomes more and more of a threat and periods of economic depression check his prosperity, he lives the sailing-captain's life that he considers the only one for a Crockett. He maintains the family mansion, and he enjoys a high scale of living. His marriage is a happy one, though it produces only one child, Nicholas. When Silas dies of a dog bite in 1864, one cannot feel sorry. The great days are past; for him to live longer would be a prolonged and increasing embitterment.

Silas' son Nicholas, because he lives only twenty-four years, is able to carry on the Crockett tradition. As a boy, he ships with his father on Eastern voyages, and as a young man he is fortunate to find berths on respectable vessels. But, unlike his father, he marries no Solace. His wife, Deborah Parsons, daughter of the headmaster of the Saturday Cove Academy, is not a bad but a willful woman with no respect for the Crockett ideals. She nags at her husband to take one of a number of good jobs offered him on steamships. She does not realize that to ask a Crockett to serve steam is like asking an artist in oils to switch to housepainting. Thus there develops a situation typical in Mary Ellen Chase's work—a clash between a man's loyalty to an ill-tempered unsympathetic wife and his loyalty to some elemental force, like the earth or the sea. We have seen it in John Peters' life in *Mary Peters;* John's ties to the soil are violated by Ellen's claims for an easy life. In the end, the land wins.

In Nicholas' case, the sea wins. But Deborah is within a hair's breadth of victory, for she is given the weapon of her pregnancy to bully her husband into high-paying work. She wields this weapon mercilessly, and Nicholas is about to succumb and take a job aboard a steamer. But a last-minute offer on one of the few remaining clippers saves him. The anger of his wife when he reveals his decision promises to be corrosive and unending. Faced with three months of quarreling at home before his ship sails from New York, he signs as one of the crew of a halibut-fishing schooner for the Grand Banks. On the Banks, "Life returned to Nicholas. . . . Order was slowly taking the place of confusion in his mind; assurance was banishing the blackness of indecision; the rightness of his allegiance was again establishing itself" (213). A few nights later Nicholas is frozen to death during his watch on the return trip to Boston. Among the

Crocketts he is the last of the deep-water sailors; and his death, though untimely, befitted his calling.

The Banks fishing that cost Nicholas his life marked a sort of interlude in the otherwise steady decline of Saturday Cove and of all but the biggest New England ports. Soon fishing became centered upon Boston, Gloucester, and Portland; and, except for lobstering and herring seining, the small communities cut their ties with the sea. Nicholas' son Reuben, born after his father's death, has no chance to continue the Crockett tradition. Yet he has immense respect for that tradition, especially as embodied in the family mansion, which is already in bad disrepair. Deserted by his mother, who had married a Boston artist, Reuben is brought up first by his grandmother Solace, who feeds his interest in family lore, and later, after Solace's death, by the old servant Susan Gray. The house is temporarily repaired with funds collected from the sale of Solace's family house to some of the summer people who are already overrunning the coast. But the respite is brief. From now on, the major conflict becomes Reuben's struggle to keep possession of his ancestral residence. To do him credit, he holds out longer than most villagers with similar encumbrances.

Yet one senses in Reuben a decline in the Crockett character. He is very steady, loyal, hard-working, honest. He is even intelligent, but he lacks the Crockett vitality and drive. Faced with the decision of whether or not to go to college to prepare himself for a life different from the customary one of his family, but perhaps as demanding and as exciting and challenging, he elects to stay at home. He bases his decision on considerations that one cannot imagine having had any influence upon his father and grandfather had they been faced with a similar situation: "To go to college meant the using of what money he had, perhaps even the mortgaging of the old house. It meant his bewildered entrance into a new and strange life among new and strange people, studies which had little appeal to him and, worst of all, the necessity for excellence if he were to succeed in any of the professions to which college inevitably led" (288).

Not all the scions of the great maritime families were so spineless. Many had gone to college and into other professions with the same enterprise, and the same success, that had goaded their forefathers to the farthest corners of the earth. In Reuben—

who, Miss Chase is at pains to tell us, is physically shorter than most Crocketts—the old stock has surely been stunted.

Yet Reuben did not, like so many Maine youths of good family, succumb to the lure of summer peoples' money and put himself at their service as a painter, a paperhanger, a mason, or a lackey. A certain residual pride sent him to the sea, first as a clerk on a coastwise steamer and, later, after a period of apprenticeship, as master. He was doing exactly the sort of thing that his grandfather at the opening of the book, had so scorned, in 1830, and he was also avoiding the labor that had cost his father his life on the Banks. Yet Miss Chase would have us keep our respect for Reuben. At least he was being sensible and adaptable, and he was still on the water. Nor was piloting a steamboat along the Maine coast really child's play. The racing tides, the innumerable reefs, shoals, and islets, the quick, thick fogs make it as difficult a stretch of coast to navigate as there is in the world. The first sailor to explore it, Samuel de Champlain, lamented that he was able to proceed only with sounding line constantly in hand; and the history of wrecks, both of steamers and sailboats in the region, would give pause to any seaman. After the terrible gale of November, 1898, which Reuben's ship survives but which causes one of the worst disasters in the history of the New England coast, the sinking of the *Portland*, with the loss of nearly two hundred lives, Reuben's respect for his calling goes up considerably.

Reuben marries a stalwart, intelligent, and good-natured schoolteacher, Huldah, who gives him one son, Silas II. But Reuben is not a child of luck, as have been so many Crocketts. Huldah, after the birth of her son, is an invalid confined to her chair for the rest of her life. Nor is Reuben's income sufficient to keep up the house. After a painful inner struggle he sells the family portraits to an art-dealer, a rather objectionable person named Schwartz whose unflattering characterization betrays Miss Chase's preference for "Anglo-Saxons." Not long afterwards Reuben is forced to sell the house itself, already heavily mortgaged, to a wealthy Philadelphia rusticator. The same year, 1930, the steamboat company suspends operations on Reuben's route. Under the stress of economic depression, Reuben is lucky and even happy to accept a job as a ferry-boat pilot in a city farther east. The ultimate humiliation has been reached in the

Crockett family: from master of a clipper ship in the China trade to ferry-boat pilot in precisely one hundred years. The water has nothing more ignoble with which to disgrace a Crockett. But the land has.

For two years young Silas, who hopes to become a physician, has been attending Bowdoin College with money from the sale of the heirlooms. Now there is no more money, and he goes to work at the dirtiest work to be found on the coast: cleaning herring in a canning factory. In offering Silas the job, Mr. Brown, the owner of the cannery, displays a blatancy not unlike that of Mr. Schwartz. After assuring Silas that he will have every opportunity to work his way up, he boasts: "The people that work in this factory aren't any Canucks or Eyetalians or even Irish. They're fine coast-of-Maine stock. Every man-jack on my rolls, and women too, has a good English name attached to him. Their families did better things years ago in these parts and in other parts of the world, too, just as yours did, I take it. But the coast has changed, I'm tellin' you, and you've got to keep pace with bad times, no matter how it gripes you" (378).

In spoofing Mr. Brown's racism, Miss Chase is making amends for the treatment she gave Mr. Schwartz, who as an antique dealer arouses her suspicion and contempt with some justification. At any rate, she pokes fun at people of her own background when she laconically remarks that, after a week of vacillation, Silas takes the job of gutting herring and stands "with the others of good English names at the first of the fish-tables" (380).

To those who know the 1930's the situation was typical enough—a man with two years in a first-rate college did the filthiest and most unskilled of jobs. There is waste in it, and tragedy. The question is: Will this last of the Crocketts survive in a capacity that in any way does honor to his name? Miss Chase leaves us somewhat in the dark, but there is hope. Silas displays a higher potential than Reuben; in him flares up some of the old vitality. True, he has forgotten or never known much of his family history. Yet deep within him he senses the presence of the past. When his fiancée, Anne Sewell, a steady, intelligent girl who bodes nothing but good for Silas' future, tells him that the past generations at least had "convictions" which persons with more scientific knowledge could not share, he bursts out:

"So have we.... All the things we've learned can't take away what's rooted in us through generations like these around us [they are standing among the Crockett graves] and through this coast and sea. Believing in a thing doesn't mean that you've got to understand all about it first" (402-3). Silas' last sentence is a rough paraphrase of a dictum of St. Anselm—*Credo ut intelligam*—that Miss Chase loves to quote and which lies apparently at the foundation of her own religious thinking.

Silas' spiritual perceptions give the best promise for his future. The early Crocketts either took their religion in their stride, or, like James's wife Abigail, gently mocked its more narrow forms. Throughout her writing Miss Chase deplores rigidity, dogmatism, and excessive zeal in religion. And throughout she praises tranquil spirituality and unostentatious Christian living. Huldah Crockett, Silas' mother, is a fine example of such a Christian. But Silas himself surpasses her in insight if not in practice. The "opening of a door," a sudden, unexpected, but unquestionably authentic experience of the presence of God, is the lot of many of Miss Chase's more fortunate characters. Silas has such perceptions. One is that just quoted, with the echoing of St. Anselm. Another occurred in his boyhood at the funeral of his grandmother, whom he had never seen alive. The minister has been reading the scriptural passages on death and resurrection:

> "Something happened to Silas as he heard the words, something more strange even than the minister's prayer. A door somewhere in his mind seemed to have swung wide open for a moment, allowing him dimly to understand that that which the minister was reading had really relatively little to do with the still figure in the coffin, that instead it had to do with all people and all things everywhere, with him and his mother and father, with days and hours, weeks and months and years, with the sun and moon and stars, with the assured faces of the Crockett men so alive on the walls, looking down at his grandmother who was dead. It was but a momentary perception. . . . but he was always to remember in after years the odd and new experience of light thus flooding his thoughts" (363-64).

It is this new facet in the Crockett character that gives one hope for the future.

Miss Chase in *Silas Crockett* has written a family chronicle, a saga, which epitomizes an era in American cultural history. The subject is an important one. The book is not merely informative entertainment for the idle hours of summer cottagers mildly curious about the past of the coast they have taken over. It is a literary monument to the endurance of the human spirit. Just as Ellen Glasgow in *Barren Ground* and in *Vein of Iron* celebrates the capacity of men and women—especially those of a proud heritage—to survive, so does Mary Ellen Chase in *Silas Crockett* and her other Maine novels celebrate the fortitude and vitality of people of similar Calvinistic background. Neither author is, of course, a Puritan; both reject the dogmas of Calvinism. Yet both admire the traits of character that are the residual legacy of Calvinism: persistence, enterprise, and above all, loyalty to a tradition—"the sacredness of tradition, the long dependence of the present upon the past" (263).

In preserving the tradition of "fortitude," as Miss Glasgow calls it, or of "acceptance rather than resignation" (83) in Miss Chase's phrase, women are most influential in the books of both authors—women like Abigail, Solace, Huldah, and Anne in *Silas Crockett*. For women more than men know that, if one endures long enough, moments of peace and security will be sure to come, "dispelling all fears, blotting them out as though they were not" (90). As is usual in Miss Chase's books, accidents, or fate, play a part in *Silas Crockett*. But Fate can be met, and is met by women like Abigail and Huldah "by the might of the human spirit reaching out toward That which had made it in the beginning" (165). In the words of the psalm, which Miss Chase quotes as the motto of *Silas Crockett*:

> As for man, his days are as grass; as a flower of the field, so he flourisheth.
>
> For the wind passeth over it, and it is gone; and the place thereof shall know it no more.
>
> But the mercy of the Lord is from everlasting to everlasting upon them that fear Him, and His righteousness unto children's children (Psalm 103).

The reception of *Silas Crockett* was all one could ask for. Since *A Goodly Heritage* Miss Chase's press has been consistently good, and her two earliest novels had been well if not enthusiastically received. As far back as *Uplands*, Theodore Morrison had praised the purity and lyricism of her style—praise which was to be repeated continuously, and justly, down to the present day. But *Mary Christmas* and *Uplands* had been mildly criticized for a tendency to "sweetness." With *A Goodly Heritage* this accusation was dropped, and lengthy reviews in most of the major periodicals praised not only the poetic beauty of her diction and sentence rhythms but the narrative skill, the evocation of atmosphere, and sociological and historical accuracy. Much the same estimates were given *Mary Peters* and *Silas Crockett*. Allan Nevins favorably compared her writing to that of Sarah Orne Jewett. R. P. T. Coffin, the Maine poet and teacher, recognized in Miss Chase the most artistic and most perceptive spokesman for the culture of his own beloved state. His commendations, as well as those of the reviewers in general, reached a climax with *Silas Crockett*. Many readers down to the present day have considered this the high point of Miss Chase's writing.

III The Edge of Darkness

Miss Chase's own favorite among all her books—not only her fiction—is the third of her Maine novels, *The Edge of Darkness,* published in 1957, twenty-two years after *Silas Crockett*. The title, which is an Eastern Maine phrase used to describe the twilight, had been in her mind for many years, and with it, undoubtedly, the germ of the book. Though superficially structureless, it is formed and framed by the death of Sarah Holt, a woman reminiscent of Sarah and Mary Peters, and Solace Crockett. Because of Sarah Holt's great age, her experiences as a young woman sailing to far parts of the world, and above all the calm spirit and the strength of character she has gained from these experiences, she dominates a tiny coastal village. The sole survivor from the seafaring days, she is the only link the villagers have with their almost forgotten heritage.

The time span of the book is the hours preceding and following Sarah's funeral. Part One presents Sarah Holt to us, mainly through the consciousness of Lucy Norton, a close friend of the old lady who has just died. Part Three describes the funeral. Part Two, the bulk of the book, consists of ten chapters which are really short stories or sketches of the lives of people who have in one way or another been influenced by Sarah, sometimes by personal contact and sometimes only by the spiritual force of her presence as a neighbor, or as a symbol, as she is described by the young doctor who attends her.

The Edge of Darkness, with its focus on a few hours of a village's life, is very different, then, from *Mary Peters,* the chronological presentation of a woman's life from childhood to late middle age, and from *Silas Crockett,* a family saga falling into four parts, each presenting a generation and each generation corresponding to a period in the decline of the coast. In style, too, *The Edge of Darkness* differs. In the other two Maine novels, there is much unabashed exposition of ideas. The author gives us her interpretation of characters and events; she philosophizes and moralizes. But *The Edge of Darkness* "is composed throughout on the principle of understatement, that is, on the desire to arouse in the reader's mind thoughts and perceptions which are purposely never allowed to appear on the pages."[6] In truth, the effect is one of brevity, without sacrifice of essential detail. The descriptions of sea, land, and village are shorter than in the previous books but no less vivid and lyrical. The characters, though we are told much less about them, become fully as alive.

The Edge of Darkness recalls, more than any of Miss Chase's other works, that masterpiece of Maine books *The Country of the Pointed Firs,* which Willa Cather in an excess of enthusiasm placed with *The Scarlet Letter* and with *Huckleberry Finn* as one of the three American books most likely to endure. Without making any such claims for *The Edge of Darkness,* we can see it has much in common with Miss Jewett's famous work. Both are accounts of remote coastal hamlets dominated by a single woman of outstanding character. Both are a series of life stories rather than a narrative of one person or family. Both present the squalid, the pitiful, as well as the colorful and heartening, sides of Maine coast life.

In *The Edge of Darkness,* Miss Chase has dwelt on the shiftlessness and decadence of many of the inhabitants of her beloved coast. Not that she had previously closed her eyes to unpleasantness; for, as far back as 1917 in a *Ladies' Home Journal* article entitled "How Four Girls 'Discovered' Maine," she wrote bluntly of the poverty, illiteracy, inbreeding, and resulting degeneracy on the Maine islands that she had visited while working for the Sea Coast Mission. But she did not, with the exception of certain passages in *Uplands,* incorporate such material into her novels until she wrote *The Edge of Darkness,* in which the chapter entitled "Backwater People" deals with as feckless a group of idlers as ever disgraced their family names. Their habitations are the once stately, but now sagging and unpainted, mansions of former shipbuilders and sea captains. Too lazy even to pick the berries that grow at their weed-choked doorsteps, they live hand to mouth from a string of inshore lobster traps or by poaching deer for the New York City market. As blind to the former glory of the coast as to the loveliness of the houses they have permitted to fall to pieces, their ideal of beauty is contained within the covers of the mail-order catalogues. Their morals are only a notch above those of Steinbeck's *paisanos;* but, unlike the *paisanos,* the sordidness of their lives is redeemed by no engagingly innocent animality.

The Backwater people are distinct from the Cove people who live on the seaward side of the peninsula, the setting of the novel. But the "Cove," though a more industrious community, is not the abode solely of virtuous happiness. Among its inhabitants are the amateur prostitute, Drusilla West; the incurable drunk, Thaddeus Holt, son of Sarah; the sour and embittered Seth and Norah Blodgett, whose marriage has congealed into unspoken hate and mute resentment. Most twisted of all is Hannah Stevens. Her sanctimonious devotion to an obscure fundamentalist sect of a type recently flourishing in the more illiterate sections of the world is a flimsy screen for a deep, angry frustration. Eventually she directs her hate against her pastor and attempts to get him fired because he has temporarily asked her to yield her place as church organist to his wife. These and other characters resemble the villagers whose warped and truncated lives filled the pages of Mary Wilkins Freeman and Rose Terry Cooke in the 1890's. Like these two, Mary Ellen Chase is bent on exhibiting the damage done to personality by a narrow existence. The winters are presented in their real harshness; the sea is as much a source of terror and hardship as a thing of beauty and a provider of livelihoods. But more destructive than sea or weather are those "more tragic disasters of estrangement and isolation" that menace so many of the Cove people and turn them "to cruel recriminations and anger, or to more cruel silence" (117).

Only very few escape these disasters. Mary Sawyer, though yet unscarred except by fear, lives in dread that her marriage will freeze into hate, as did that of her parents, Nora and Seth Blodgett. Lobster fisherman Samuel Parker, a bachelor, when not on the water, annihilates time in tidying and dusting his three immaculate rooms and, when this obsessive occupation fails him, in playing solitary word games; he finds only partial fulfillment in several close friendships. The restrictions of his life have made him immune, to be sure, to the common calamities, but they have also made him indifferent to the larger human realizations. Of all the dwellers "in that lonesome cove on that God-forsaken point of land" (122), as those who lived "away" called the village, the least frustrated are Lucy and Joel Norton, who keep the local general store. Lucy in particular is able to find meaning in life—something more than mere submission to a routine like Samuel Parker's. Partly she owes this fulfillment to her occupation as a shopkeeper, which brings her into contact with many people and keeps her at least healthily busy. But more important has been her close friendship with Sarah Holt, whose wisdom and completeness of spirit have irradiated Lucy's existence.

Among the villagers Lucy had been closest to Sarah and had been most influenced by her. An incredibly long and adventurous life—the end of which marks the end of an era on the coast, as the doctor says—had equipped Sarah with a set of defenses to meet most irritations and tragedies. Lucy Norton has strengthened herself from this same armory. From Sarah she has learned the most valuable lessons for withstanding the erosions and corrosions of daily living, whether in a metropolis or a hamlet: "that malice and charity, tenderness and cruelty, pettiness and nobility can exist almost at the same hour in most human hearts. She was, in addition, quite able, with regret, but with humor, to detect them likewise within her own" (83). She has learned from Sarah Holt not "to expect so much of folks . . . and especially of seafaring folks. The sea's a rough master. It brings out the best a man has, and yet it has a queer way of nourishing the worst" (84). And finally she has learned from Sarah Holt what is perhaps the ultimate in wisdom: "Nothing's for always, thank God" (84).

Some hours before the funeral, Lucy Norton visits Sarah's

cottage, where the body lies awaiting the earth: "What she had come for and foolishly had expected to find here alone with Sarah, until her mind had defeated her, was the seizure, if only for a moment, of the meaning of Sarah Holt's long, hard triumphant life. If she could only grasp that meaning. . . ." (18). She does not, cannot, grasp it in its entirety; but she comes close to grasping it, at the end of the book, on the evening after the funeral. In one of those moments of insight experienced by one or two characters in almost all of Mary Ellen Chase's books, Lucy Norton sees the world and mankind in oneness—fishermen on remote shores of England, Iceland, Norway, living out their lives of obscure toil to the rhythms of the ebbing and flowing tides and the setting and rising sun—and she is filled with "admiration and wonder that men and women were what they were, insignificant, unknown, and yet invincible in what Sarah Holt had called the circle of life. There was wonder, too, as in this hour, in these strange returns of faith, which, unbidden and even unexpected, now and then enclosed the human spirit, shutting out fears, redeeming one's place and time, making possible one's future" (232-33).

The meaning of Sarah Holt's life, then, is the one with which all great literature endows the lives of its heroes, whether kings or peasants, who exist and die in harmony with the eternal laws of God and nature. It is not to be grasped by reason but by intuition, faith. But for all its elusiveness, it is the most real of all meanings. It is a meaning, moreover, that on the day of Sarah's funeral affects, however fleetingly, not only Lucy but all those who attend and who have known Sarah. For a few moments, at least, their lives take on a new dimension: that of eternity, which is ever a dimension of the present for those fortunate enough to see beneath the surface. Tomorrow, of course, the Cove people would be much the same as they always had been: "They would be drawn apart . . . each intent upon his own existence, each caught and held within his own snares, woven from the past or constantly entangled by the present" (222). But Sarah Holt's life—and death—has given all their lives a moment of significance; has added for a moment to their stature by making them spiritual beings. For this purpose Sarah Holt has lived; for this purpose we all live, but few of us fulfill ourselves so successfully.

The twenty-two years between the publication of *The Edge of Darkness* and the second of the Maine novels, *Silas Crockett*, correspond roughly with the lapse of time between *The White Gate* and *A Goodly Heritage* and the parts of *A Goodly Fellowship* which deal with Maine. *The White Gate* is briefer, psychologically profounder, and more lyrical than its predecessors. The same may be said of *The Edge of Darkness*, which was published within three years of *The White Gate*. Miss Chase's perceptions had sharpened, and her control of her material had tightened. But the intervening period had been rich in productivity—three novels, two biographies, two books on the Bible, not to mention lesser works—nor did the output fall off after *The Edge of Darkness*. We must turn now to this impressive body of material and examine it by genre, including that of children's books, down to the present day. We shall consider first those of her novels which she excluded from the Maine category, i. e., those whose chief concern is not the evocation of the life and spirit of her native state, though their setting may in part be there. The first of these is the short novel, *Dawn in Lyonesse*, published in 1938.

CHAPTER 5

Novels of England and America

I Dawn in Lyonesse: *Release into Timelessness*

WISDOM—that is, liberation of mind from the prison of daily circumstance—dawns on us as an awareness of the past and a perception of the meaning with which the past invests one's life: this is the theme of Miss Chase's novella *Dawn in Lyonesse*. Such wisdom is slow in invading our consciousness, in breaking down the walls of our captivity. To describe its advent, Miss Chase quotes, as the motto of the book, from E. A. Robinson's *Tristram*. Isolt of Brittany is speaking to her father King Howel. Isolt has just heard of the death of her husband, Tristram, who had loved not her but the other Isolt, wife of King Mark. She says:

> Wisdom is not one word and then another,
> Till words are like dry leaves under a tree;
> Wisdom is like a dawn that comes up slowly
> Out of an unknown ocean.

The setting of Miss Chase's story is Tintagel and Land's End in present-day Cornwall, country which she loved and had come to know well on her frequent visits to England. Cornwall is, of course, part of the West Country, and is adjacent to Thomas Hardy's Wessex. In a book of essays, *This England*, published in 1938, she records at length her knowledge of the West Country, which she considers the most scenic in England and the most English in the character and customs of its people. Furthermore, among them she finds the same fatalism and superstitions that are evident among the peasants in Hardy's novels. Tess of the D'Urbervilles gets inklings of her tragic destiny from such incidents as the reluctance of her cows to give down their milk, the failure of butter to form in the churn, or the rustle of ivy leaves at her window. Similarly, the heroine of *Dawn in Lyonesse,* Ellen Pascoe, interprets the entry of a bird into a house as an augury of death. And she believes that, if one crawls through a hole in a certain rock at Land's End and makes a wish, the wish will come true.

Ellen Pascoe, a servant girl in a Tintagel hotel, is soon to marry the fisherman Derek Tregonny, whose years of strain in World War I have made him an introvert, shutting him off from full participation in the joys and sorrows of life. Ellen, too, has been withdrawn and unhappy, enduring life in a series of jobs as barmaid and fish gutter. But she has slowly awakened to the past of Cornwall and to the story of the mythical land of Lyonesse, now sunk beneath the sea save for a few jagged monoliths that are a perennial challenge to archeologists. The legend of Tristram and Iseult, which she has read in a red book kept in the lounge of the hotel where she works, has awakened her imagination and transformed her emotional life.

The lost land of Lyonesse, Miss Chase clearly intends, represents the past; and the monoliths, jutting above the waters of the ocean that engulfs all memory, are what remain of the past in our present lives. Yet these excrescences from prehistory may exert a strong influence on us. The legends of her race and country obtrude themselves into Ellen's workaday world. No longer does she see things in their old humdrum, hopeless light. The potentialities of her existence expand beyond measurement.

Ellen's knowledge of Mark and Tristram and the two Iseults, gleaned from the red book at night after a long day's work and supplemented from her conversations with an American professor to whom she daily serves breakfast, has a twofold effect upon her. It adds excitement to her own love affair, which hitherto had seemed drab to her, and also gives it a meaning it could not have had without her new knowledge. But it gives her doubts too about her future with a man who has experienced no such awakening as hers. Yet her joy in her own escape from the meaninglessness of the particular into the significance of the universal—a true religious awakening—outweighs her fears. The throbbing, crashing waves beneath the cliffs at Tintagel speak to her now of other lives in other millennia—lives that have pulsed to the same waves of ecstasy and despair that she has known. Her discovery of the cave where Tristram and Iseult had made love translates her to the realms of poetry. Her lifelong habit of awakening for a short time just before dawn now brings her an exultant sense of timelessness. For such released spirits as hers, "it is in this earliest hour, the dawn before dawn, that life is most fully lived, life unworried by time, life before which time creeps, submissive and humble, shorn of its power. Life now is not time, nor time life.... Years and months, days and hours, become only the brittle, empty shells of life from which its glowing radiance is freed to lighten the darkness of time itself, to confound it with wisdom and understanding. In this one hour time is salvaged, the imperishable taken from it and seen without disguise" (12-13).

But Ellen's love, like that of the legendary lovers who have so enthralled her imagination, comes to a tragic end. A sudden catastrophe, inevitable in Miss Chase's novels, shatters Ellen's hopes and dispels her fears. Derek commits suicide by drowning. After attending his funeral, Ellen learns the reason from a barmaid, Susan Pengilly, her best and lifelong friend. During Ellen's absence in Tintagel, Susan, desperate for marriage, had seduced Derek, who had spent on her the money he was saving for his marriage to Ellen. After some time, he becomes so overwhelmed by guilt that he ends his life.

Over Derek's death hovers an ironic fatalism, not lost on the superstitious girls. Susan sorrowfully confesses that in the early spring she had crawled through the hole in the monolith at Land's End and her wish had been that Derek would never marry Ellen. The wish had been granted, but not as she had hoped. Ellen also recalls that she had asked the American archeologist at her hotel to make a wish for her at the same stone. Her wish was that Derek, before he married her, would learn the same things she had learned; that he would escape from captivity in the present with its agonies of selfhood, into the broader, freer regions where past, present, and future co-exist. This wish, too, has been granted; for, as she learns from Susan, Derek had at last broken loose from the web of pain in which he had floundered since the war and, most marvelous of all, he had begun, as Susan put it, "to say things like in books —after I'd done wrong in asking 'im to love me. I can't forget the things 'e said.... 'E laughed different, too. 'Twas like 'e 'ad come out of a prison" (105-6).

The completeness of Ellen's own release into timelessness now becomes clear. Were she still a captive of circumstance, she would have quarreled violently with Susan and hated her for life. But, seeing her own tragedy in the perspective of the past, she feels pity rather than hate. She perceives in her own misfortunes the perennial human lot. She is not alone, battling her grief like someone floundering in the depths of a well. She is living through events that men and women have been living through for countless centuries. For companionship she has all humanity. And so she rises to the ultimate summit of freedom—the freedom that comes with forgiveness.

That night at Land's End after the funeral and after her friend's confession, she again awakes a little before dawn and again she finds herself under the dominion of time. But not for long; she knows: "The nearer past built a wall between her and those long years that had gone, and she could not see beyond it. Yet there must be other dawns, she thought, hours which would give back to her the deathless things which she had known" (115). And, even at this moment of seeming setback, she thinks again of Tristram and realizes that, like him, she too has lived life to the full. She knows that healing cannot be too far in the future.

Dawn in Lyonesse is an affirmation of the limitless potential latent in the human soul, even that of a servant girl. In no less a degree than Mary Peters, Ellen has made the discovery that life, even for the humblest, may be a miraculous adventure of the spirit. To some it comes as a heightened religious awareness; to others, as to Ellen, it comes as a consciousness of the past, an acceptance of the legacy offered by the place of one's birth. The fact that it is from a book that Ellen first learns and feels the strength of the past of her native Cornwall is a tribute to literature that one would expect from Miss Chase, who herself had found much of the meaning of her own life from books and had spent most of her life teaching them to the young. The ultimate use of literature, Miss Chase would say, is not solely to enrich but to transform our lives. *Dawn in Lyonesse* records such a transformation.

Dawn in Lyonesse is itself a prose poem—one of the most lyrical of Miss Chase's books. The story does not closely parallel that of Tristram and Iseult, but it borrows some of the poetry of that most romantic of medieval tales. Derek, wounded in spirit, is cured by Susan, just as Tristram, wounded in body, is cured by Iseult of Ireland. In both cases the love eventuates in death—the *liebestod* motif. Except for a number of quotations from various versions of the legend, this is the extent of Miss Chase's debt. The style is that of a prose poem. The sentences have a rhythmic sweep like that of the Cornish surf. The diction is vividly image-making. Miss Chase is at her best in describing Cornwall, that region where, as in her native Maine, sea and land are mingled, sometimes in tempestuous strife, sometimes in halcyon partnership, but never without a grandeur and a beauty that dominate the lives of those who live and die there. The symbolic overtones of the geography have already been mentioned—the land lost beneath the ocean from which the jagged peninsula slants up as the present slopes up from the past. On the cliff near Land's End stands the church where Derek's funeral takes place: an ancient building fronting the implacable breakers, from whose square tower on stormy nights a lamp is burnt to guide belated mariners—just as Faith itself, with roots deep in the past, is a light to storm-lost souls.

P. H. Boynton in *America in Contemporary Fiction* has justly remarked that in *Dawn in Lyonesse* Miss Chase's "deftness in narration and characterization is exercised to its highest degree" (25). It is indeed almost a perfect short novel—one that ranks in economy of structure and singleness of effect with the very best novellas that American writers have produced—those of James, Melville, and Willa Cather. Like many good novellas it gave promise of making an effective play, but as dramatized by Thomas Job and presented at the Playhouse in New York on December 11, 1947, it flopped. According to a post mortem by Rosamond Gildes in *Theatre Arts* (February, 1947) *Land's End,* as it was called, suffered from overproduction, gimcrack staging, too-sophisticated costumes, and caterwauling music. A review in the *New Yorker* (December 24, 1946) was no more complimentary.

Miss Chase herself converted *Dawn in Lyonesse* into the short story "A Candle at Night," printed in *Collier's* of May 9, 1942. In it she employed the same basic plot, but changed the names of the characters. Many sentences and paragraphs are almost verbatim transcriptions from the novel. The dialogue is often the same, though she has tamed down the Cornish dialect for the benefit of a mass American readership. Most regrettable is the loss of the theme of liberation of self through an awareness of the human lot as it has been lived through the ages—a liberation that enables one to forgive even his betrayer. In "A Candle at Night" the forgiveness remains, but the antecedent liberation is all but absent, perhaps because of limitations of space in which to trace its development. Many an author has successfully expanded a short story to a novel or novella, as Miss Chase herself did in writing *Uplands.* This strange reversal of the usual procedure had regrettable results.

II Windswept

An important theme in *Mary Peters* and *Silas Crockett,* we have seen, is the perpetuation of spiritual values in the midst of change. The change is that which transformed the Maine coast from a closely knit maritime culture whose ships were at home in the ports and oceans of the world into a fishing and finally into a resort area ignominiously dependent upon the patronage of well-to-do Bostonians, New Yorkers, and Philadelphians. The older generation had been proud in an independence as complete as the conditions of global commerce would permit. The later generation was still proud, but its pride accorded poorly with its function of catering to the summer visitors. The outward signs of change were the disappearance first of the sailing ships and later of the coastwise steamers and the advent of the railroad and the automobile. The inner signs were a narrowing of the spirit, a diminishing of ambition, a meanness of thought and imagination.

The spiritual foundation of the older culture had been that of New England Calvinism made tolerant—and tolerable—by contact with the cultures of the outer world. The Puritan values and virtues were all there: devotion to duty and hard work, emphasis on education and learning, a God-fearing and Bible-centered piety, family solidarity. But on the Maine coast these qualities, which elsewhere frequently degenerated into a gloomy bigotry, were humanized by a sense of the joy and excitement of life imported from sunnier climes and happier civilizations. At their best, the Maine coast inhabitants had a talent for life—

a versatility, a balance between seriousness and joyousness not shared by the more orthodox Puritans of earlier times or more inland locales. Miss Chase obviously believes that a society thrives only when brought into contact with other and differing societies. If Maine escaped becoming ingrown like colonial Salem or nineteenth-century back-country New England, it was because of such contacts. In *Mary Christmas* and in *Uplands* Mary Ellen Chase describes the intrusion of new blood—new nationalities and new religions—into Maine, and the result of such graftings is usually beneficial. In *Windswept* she pursues the same theme but on a broader scale. At present she is planning a novel on the Poles in America. Thirty-seven years after *Mary Christmas* she feels the need to champion the immigrant. Many Americans, especially politicians, have often taken the stand that only the "Americanism" of third- or fourth-generation, or older, citizens is desirable or even acceptable. Theodore Roosevelt made the classic statement of this view in his essay "What Americanism Means," which has been reprinted in innumerable anthologies and textbooks. His recommendation, quite brutally stated, was that the newly arrived immigrant immediately shed his old habits, ideas, ideals, attitudes, loyalties, and language. To do anything less than to consign the old ways to the ash can and to adopt those of the old-line English and Dutch segments of the population was, Roosevelt implied, ample grounds for deportation. Owing to its jingoistic patness, its widespread dissemination through the schools, and the fame of the author himself, Roosevelt's views on the duties of immigrants were accepted by the general public including the newcomers themselves, to whom, in the second generation at least, anything smacking of the old country was considered a matter for shame.

In literature, this brand of chauvinism had occasionally been espoused, even before Roosevelt's utterance, as by Thomas Bailey Aldrich in his notorious "Danger at the Gates." But most writers did not succumb either to Aldrich's phobia or to Roosevelt's smugness. Writers in America—indeed in most healthy societies—have fortunately been nonconformists. Most vocal in befriending the immigrant as a contributor to American civilization was Willa Cather, who was a personal friend of Miss Chase and whose works Miss Chase greatly admires. In novel after novel Willa Cather demonstrated the enrichment that America owed to the cultures, languages, and religions of its immigrants. Her Swedish, Russian, Bohemian homesteaders, far from discarding their heritage at Ellis Island, retained it and flourished with it on the Western plains. Like Virgil's Aeneas carrying his lares and penates to the new land of Italy, these settlers brought their old-world tradition to civilize the new land. Fusion with older American ways inevitably occurred, and both cultures, the old and the new, were the gainers. Sometimes the immigrant contribution was mainly religious; for example, Roman Catholicism functions as a vehicle of civilization in *Death Comes for the Archbishop* and in *Shadows on the Rock.* Sometimes it was a peasant tradition of hard labor and love of the soil, as in *My Antonia.* But always the new country is transformed. The new land needs a culture as well as a people, and the two must necessarily come together.

Windswept invites comparison with Miss Cather's immigrant novels. For *Windswept* too deals with a newcomer to America and with the settlement of the newcomer and an old-line American, working together, on a tract of wilderness land. On an uninhabited stretch of the eastern Maine coast, Philip Marston, a Maine boy who has made a success in New York as a marine engineer, dreams of building a house for himself and his descendants. The location is a vast sweep of high shoreline, such as Miss Chase knew at Petit Manan Point, where she spent sixteen summers in her cottage "Windswept," the name she later gave to her novel and to Philip's house. Philip has long felt the need to sink roots somewhere, both for his own sake and for his son's. His Maine childhood had been made unhappy by his uncompromisingly conventional and unsympathetic mother. His marriage too has proved to be unhappy. He wishes to establish for himself and his descendants a tradition of their own; and, recognizing that place is always important in a tradition, he selects a locality in his native state but at a safe distance from the scene of his dreary upbringing.

From the very beginning a co-partner in the enterprise is Jan Pisek, a Bohemian immigrant whom Marston had befriended on his arrival in the United States. Like Willa Cather's immigrants, Jan is of peasant stock. He is kind, hard-working, shrewd, in harmony with the tranquillity of the soil, loyal, and endowed with spiritual resources that stem from a devout

Catholicism. His capacity for friendship is unlimited. All these qualities he brings to America. Symbolic of this heritage is a packet of his native soil that he intends to have mingled with the American soil that will sometime cover his grave.

We have repeatedly been reminded of the importance that Miss Chase sees in good and meaningful memories from childhood. Such memories are the only sure foundation for wholeness of personality during adult life. Philip Marston's purpose at "Windswept," like that of the Marstons who live there later, is to assure such saving memories for each generation; for American life elsewhere, especially in the cities, has somehow failed to provide them. Jan is invaluable in this purpose because he lives by memories brought from the old country—memories not only of his own lifetime but ones handed down from earlier generations: "In Jan's mind a man dwelt by himself within himself, in an impregnable stronghold of old loyalties, within which stronghold he was the guardian of old gifts, the suffering and the sacrifice of countless others, long since gone but never lost, toil and privation, defeats and triumphs, fears and hopes. A man was thus the inheritor and the guardian alike of time, its guerdons and its punishments. Within him was the long past, the confusing present, the uncharted future. If this stronghold were stormed and overcome, a man was lost, set adrift, his identity scattered into fragments . . ." (113-14).

To Jan the present is "but a meeting of the past with the future" (186). Once one loses the past, one loses the present and the future as well. This is what happens to Jan's good friend Anton, who was from Jan's own Bohemian village and had come to America on the same ship. The two set up a profitable shoe-repair shop in New York. Jan strives "to keep untouched and secure those old realities which he and Anton had known, the burden and the brightness of those old years in an old land. . . . to keep alive in Anton the decencies of poverty and hard work and waiting, the desire to be true to old and simple faiths, the wish to remember in all the temptation to forget" (113). But, while Jan deals in centuries, "Anton deal[s] in hours" (113). Anton forfeits his country's and his childhood's past. His life disintegrates. He forges a check and serves a term in jail. "To forget good things does bad things to a man" (368).

What makes a man forget? Modern mechanical and urban civilization is partly to blame. Philip Marston feels the need of establishing himself at "Windswept" precisely because his New York life is fragmentary and chaotic. Furthermore, perhaps as a concomitant of chaos, his marriage has been heading toward disaster, and he feels spiritually isolated from his times. There is nothing to do but begin afresh on a piece of virgin land in partnership with a man like Jan whose life is whole.

On the day he gets title to the land at Windswept, Philip Marston is shot in a hunting accident. But Philip's fourteen-year-old son, John, insists on having the house built and on living there, first out of respect for his father's wishes, later as the expression of a deeply cherished philosophy of life, which resembles Miss Chase's and which she presents sometimes in his words and thoughts, sometimes through Jan's, and sometimes as author's commentary on the action.

Much of John's philosophy is derived from Jan, who remains continuously at "Windswept" from the year it is built. From Jan he learns that "a man's roots mattered . . . his identification with a given place which might well serve as an anchor to windward against the storms of time and chance" (243). John Marston, like his father, mistrusts technological civilization. He has visions of vast conflicts in the future—wars that engulf humanity in the course of the book and cost him his son and his daughter's fiancée—"brought upon the world by this very mechanical skill, this power of invention. . . . It was to fortify themselves against such monstrous possibilities that he wanted roots for his children, put far down in old, sturdy soil, the soil, first of all, of some actual place, benevolent, even sacred to those who had gone before them, the soil also of discovered realities and values" (244).

It is from such soil that Jan springs and that Jan finds again at "Windswept" after a period of uprooted life in New York. At "Windswept" his life "returned to its old continuity which his years in New York had broken, spanned those years, stretching across them the broken strands of the past, knitting those securely to the stout threads of the present. Now warp and woof could once more be woven into an invincible fabric, old days, old years, new hours, new sights and sounds, old and new thoughts" (214).

Thus old-line American and the immigrant alike need spiritual roots plunging deeply in time and place; this is a cardinal point in Miss Chase's point of view. The immigrant's most valuable contribution to a new land is his possession of a tradition which needs only the proper soil for successful transplanting. Far from breaking with his old-world past, as Theodore Roosevelt would have had him do, Jan cherishes it—its religion, its language, its peasant strength and virtues, even its prejudices against Germans. The fruits of the transplanted tradition may be shared, if only by the example of spiritual integrity, with his new fellow countrymen. Without Jan Pisek and later his sister Philomena, "Windswept" would not have been a seedbed of character and enduring values.

On this general foundation, Philip Marston, who devotes his life to translation and literary scholarship, erected an educational philosophy which restates what Mary Ellen Chase has been saying in most of her works but especially in *A Goodly Fellowship.* Recollecting in his musings Dr. Johnson's famous dictum that "between the lettered and the unlettered man . . . there is as much difference as between the living and the dead" (240), John Marston phrases a dictum of his own: "life without conscious associations is not life but death" (240), a principle perfectly illustrated in the life of Ellen Pascoe in *Dawn in Lyonesse.* But these associations need not come from books, as Dr. Johnson had assumed. To the scholar, the sea, the trees, the bees, might suggest Virgil, but men like Jan had never heard of Virgil. To Jan, living is a creative process in that he ceaselessly orients his daily actions to the traditions of which he is an embodiment. In his life the outward and the visible are constantly being transmuted into the inward and the spiritual. Jan is capable of this miraculous transformation, which is so essential to the true success of our lives, because he had learned as a child, that the quality of our acts—their right motives—is more important than the profit or loss they bring us personally. Thus, "in poverty he had found wealth; in simplicity, splendour; in labour, patience and wisdom . . ." (240-41). The lives of persons like Jan provide existence with its ultimate meanings, reduce chaos to form and symmetry, point the way to release from the tyranny of things.

In Jan's life we have a perfect example of what we really mean by education, the building of mind and spirit, the continuous, "often unconscious, rescue within oneself of life from death, beginning long before one was aware of it in the associations made possible through the places in which one found oneself, through the persons one knew . . . the books one read and loved" (241).

With its emphasis on the transmutation of the outward and visible into the inward and spiritual, this theory is squarely in the Christian tradition. But it is also suggestive, very likely not intentionally on Miss Chase's part, of the Hinduism of the Gita, which preaches detachment from the fruits of action. The idea that we may defeat death through the transmutation of symbols, or associations, into spiritual reality, brings to mind, moreover, some of Boris Pasternak's most impressive passages on immortality. But when Marston muses that the most important of all the "sources of life," i.e., associations, is the "accident of place" (241), the determinism of Hardy or of the Naturalists receives its recognition.

Place being so crucial, the majestic landscape of "Windswept" is central to the book. It is the hub from which radiate the spokes which give strength to the Marston family life all along its circumference. But neither Philip nor John neglects the other sources of life-giving associations. From John onward all the boys attend St. Paul's School at Concord, New Hampshire, noted in real life for its Classical and religiously oriented education. At "Windswept" John builds a chapel, complete with altar, bell, and burying ground. And he brings to "Windswept" on long visits persons whole in spirit who refill rather than drain the reservoirs of life there. Often these are servants: Jan, of course, and his sister Philomena; but also the Maine carpenter Caleb Perkins, whose work is that of an artist; and the housekeeper Mrs. Haskell, whose earthy Maine presence suggests qualities of ancient Greece and the Holy Land. Like Sarah Orne Jewett's Elmiry Todd, "her stout percale and gingham skirts might have swept the asphodel and thyme of Grecian hillsides, the lilies of Judean fields. If they had been put upon her, she might have played the parts of Hecuba or Antigone or of Judith, the widow of Manasses, and comported herself as well as they had done down the long reaches of the world" (223).

Most impressive of the outsiders brought into the orbit of "Windswept" is Mother Radegund, superior of a French convent on the Hudson River, whose admiration for John Marston's translation of François Villon leads her to seek his friendship. Mother Radegund is a flower of Catholicism, cultured, tolerant, urbane, efficient, devout. Perhaps she is modeled after the nuns at St. Catherine's in Minnesota whom Miss Chase so much admired. She entrusts to John the guardianship of her niece's out-of-wedlock daughter, fathered by a man dead in the war and born in the convent shortly after the Armistice. "Windswept," though Protestant, seems to Mother Radegund the most promising haven she can find for the little girl, and her estimate is correct. Julie flourishes there, growing into an intelligent and sensitive young woman, apparently destined to marry Rod, the child of John's old age, if he survives World War II, which begins one day after the close of the novel.

Though *Windswept* is set for the most part in Maine, Miss Chase does not consider it one of her "Maine novels," for it does not deal primarily with indigenous coastal people nor with peculiarly coastal problems. But in structure, that of a family chronicle, it resembles *Mary Peters* and *Silas Crockett*. *Windswept* covers a period of sixty years, from 1880 to 1939. In it the lives of three generations of Marstons are recorded. The plot is episodic rather than complex. The descriptions of the Maine coast are accurate and lyrical. Published in 1941, it went through fifteen reprintings by 1952. At least one reviewer, Robert Hillyer, writing in the *Atlantic* of December, 1941, considered it Miss Chase's best novel to that date. All reviewers praised its beautiful prose. Its popularity with the public may have been due to its undisguised attempt to diagnose the sickness of our times when that sickness had erupted into the most disastrous war in history. Upheaval, rootlessness, displacement are all bywords of the century. Not only does Miss Chase focus on these symptoms but she attempts to prescribe for their eradication.

Windswept has weaknesses as a novel; it is almost obtrusively didactic, a fault Miss Chase escaped in her Maine novels, especially in *The Edge of Darkness;* it is excessively "sweet" in places; the plot, which brings together such a diversity of persons on a remote section of the coast, uncomfortably stretches the imagination. Yet it is an eminently readable book and a serious one. Its wisdom will not attract those among our intellectuals who feel that an idea must be new, exotic, or spectacular to deserve consideration. Beatniks, Existentialists, angry young men and women will be appalled by the, to them, superficiality of Miss Chase's thought. But the fact remains that the open-minded reader, however much he may disagree, cannot casually dismiss this book. It approaches the much-touted "human predicament" as forthrightly as does an Existentialist. Violence, crime, chance, war, failure all play a part in it. The way of life that Miss Chase points out is not an easy one. Like Mother Radegund, she desires "not that sin might be spared its bitter fruits, not that life might be quickened and restored, but that all humanity might learn to pity itself and thus to understand, might some day want above all else to bind up the broken-hearted, to proclaim deliverance to those that were captive, to open the prisons to those that were bound.... *De profundis clamavi ad te, Domine, Domine, exaudi vocem meam*" (344-45).

As for the political state of the modern world, Miss Chase sums it up in John Marston's words spoken just before World War II: "You can't build a safe future with hatred and revenge and blindness on one side of the ocean and with people following false Gods on the other" (388). Nowhere in *Windswept* is there an easy optimism. Man can anchor himself in a tradition, can shore up his present and future with good memories of the past. But there is no safeguard against accident and heartbreak, death and disaster. Mary Ellen Chase leaves no doubt about this. The novel begins with a prologue laid in Nazi-swept Central Europe in September, 1938; it ends on August 31, 1939.

III The Plum Tree

The Plum Tree, published by Macmillan in 1949, reads like a fiction for *Ladies' Home Journal*—skillful, suspenseful, mildly witty, with more than a touch of folksiness. Miss Chase's reputation certainly has not been benefited by writing *The Plum Tree;* but it has not been damaged, for she is incapable of an incompetent job. The theme is a valid one and typical: stored within us we have energies and endurance which we realize are there only when they well forth in some serious emergency. The source of this strength, Miss Chase implies, is in the experiences of our early lives—again a valid and typical idea.

Emma Davis, R.N., one of two middle-aged spinsters who run an efficient and humane home for aged ladies, is the heroine of the tale. She is kindly, sensible, persevering:

> Emma Davis had not forgotten—anything. She had not forgotten the terror or the despair or the sadness, nor yet the gaiety, the courage, and the faith of forty years spent with illness, old age, and death. Only in some odd way, through those many years, she had been able, though quite unconsciously, to transcend experience itself into the meaning of it, to capture and hold the essence, the quality, and the spirit of experience, which in comparison with the mere recollection of events and circumstances, is the rare miracle of memory, the possible daily changing of water into wine, and within which is healing rather than pain" (14-15).

As the story begins, Emma Davis is faced with the task of removing to the State Hospital three old ladies suffering from psychoses. One, a massive Swedish woman, threatens to murder someone, anyone, with a bread knife at precisely four o'clock of a certain afternoon. Another is convinced she is going to die at the same hour on the same day and has attempted to telephone an undertaker to arrange for the picking up of her corpse. A third has made preparations to return, again at four o'clock of the same day, to her home that has been demolished for years. The situation, in truth, is more trying for Miss Davis than believable for the reader. The climax—a tea party at which Miss Davis entertains the madwomen until, exactly at four in the afternoon of the fated day, a car arrives to carry them all to the State Hospital—is less suspenseful than it would have been under less incredible circumstances. The plot is redeemed only by the irony with which Miss Chase treats her characters. For our psychoanalytic age the causes of the three psychoses are not, however, sufficiently accounted for, except perhaps that of the homicidal Swede, whose life, we are told, had been shattered by homesteading on the Great Plains beneath the menacing shadows of the Rocky Mountains.

Almost as contrived as the four o'clock climax is the function of the plum tree blooming on the grounds of the old ladies' home. The whiteness of the tree, to be sure, suggests the purity of heart that Kierkegaard equates with singleness of purpose. Certainly Emma Davis and her partner have been guided by one humane purpose to which all else—travel, wealth, perhaps marriage—has been sacrificed. From self-denial stems their purity and their strength. As suggestive of this, the tree is effective. But a bit too mechanical is its use as a catalyst to precipitate in Emma's consciousness the memories which release her energies for the ordeal she faces. The connection between the tree and the memories is often too tenuous for credence even under the broadest interpretation of the principle of association of ideas.

Miss Chase places her story in "a fair-sized American town, and yet it might equally well be placed in London or in Amsterdam, in Rome or in Reykjavik, in Calcutta or in Jerusalem" (1). In the vagueness of setting lies the fundamental weakness of the novel. Unplaced fiction tends to become overgeneralized; that is, it becomes allegorical. And, except in the hands of adepts like Bunyan and Swift, allegory is liable to be mechanical. Even Tolstoy's parables are rooted in peasant life and the Russian countryside, a fact which makes them alive as stories in addition to conveying a moral lesson. Mary Ellen Chase's talent for evoking place is one of her major assets. Her not bringing that ability to bear in *The Plum Tree* necessitates her resort to devices that weaken the story.

Her failure to localize *The Plum Tree* is all the more regrettable because Emma Davis is a New England woman, and her presence outside the United States in any of the cities Miss Chase mentions would be highly unlikely except in Calcutta, where she might be serving as a missionary. Individually, her cardinal qualities of endurance, faithfulness, and ingenuity, and her Emersonian bent of spiritualizing the material circumstances of her life could, of course, be found anywhere. So perhaps might her lesser qualities of ironic humor tending to understatement, a longing to travel, a self-indulgence that despite her sense of duty permits her to enjoy a crying jag, a wild ride on a bicycle, or even a bout of drinking. But all these traits, both lesser and major, as combined in Emma Davis add up to only one thing: a Yankee woman who in the fictional world might have stepped out of the pages of Sarah Orne Jewett, William Dean Howells, or Henry James, and in real life could be found in any area of the United States dominated by New England culture and ideas. Other cultures undoubtedly have the equivalent of Emma Davis but not the duplicate.

IV The Lovely Ambition

Unlike *The Plum Tree,* Mary Ellen Chase's last novel, *The Lovely Ambition,* published by Norton in 1960, does celebrate the importance of place, thus taking its position in the mainstream of her writing. Certain places, Miss Chase believes, are endowed with a unique spirit which reveals itself to certain persons in a strange but real way, even casting a spell over them. One such place is the East Anglian town of Bury St. Edmunds, which exerts a magnetism on the hero of *The Lovely Ambition,* the Methodist preacher, John Tillyard. Obviously the same area and city have also cast a spell over Miss Chase, for she yearly visits Cambridge and, while writing *Silas Crockett,* lived two years in nearby Grantchester, both within a few miles of Bury St. Edmunds. But despite this fascination, Parson Tillyard has long dreamed of emigrating to America. He has been deeply impressed by De Tocqueville's account of the democracy beyond the sea, and he reads Thoreau's *Walden* as if it were scripture. The son of a farmer and a "chapel" preacher in an area where the "Church," or Anglicanism, has prestige, Tillyard has come to regard America as a land where the human mind is respected for what it may become; a land where one can practice his own form of worship and pursue his own way of life free from discrimination. Until the end of his life, though he returns to England, he retains his high opinion of America and almost his last words are an expression of hope that America, caught up in her great surge of prosperity, "will never become careless and indifferent to her particular ideal of freedom" (287).

When an American bishop visiting England offers John Tillyard a parish in eastern Maine, he decides to go; he takes with him, of course, his wife and three children—Mary, the oldest; the twins, Ansie and the girl (her name is never given) who narrates the story. After a harrowing transatlantic passage in steerage, where they see humanity exhibiting the worse of its propensity for dirt and brawling selfishness, they settle down in the Maine-coast village of Pepperel, under the care of the efficient, motherly housekeeper, Mrs. Baxter. The parson flourishes. He acquires a horse, a cow, and some sheep. He visits Walden Pond, which, next to Bury St. Edmunds, is to him the most hallowed spot on earth. He becomes a visiting chaplain at the State Hospital in Augusta, and later invites some of the inmates to his home to share the peace of his own life. The children and his wife also flourish until one day the fatal accident that one expects in a novel by Mary Ellen Chase shatters the harmony of their existence. Ansie, now a student at Philips Exeter Academy, is killed in a haying mishap on his father's farm, just as was Jarvis Craig, the hero of *Uplands*. The accident occurs not only at the fullness of the harvest but at the fullness of the family's life together. The parents and younger daughter return to England for a short visit, leaving Mary behind to attend a college in Massachusetts; but the visit prolongs itself into permanency. The two girls, however, who are rather thoroughly Americanized, receive their education in American colleges and subsequently live in America.

In her portrayal of John Tillyard, Miss Chase has set herself the challenging task of bringing to life a man who lives almost entirely in the spirit. He is, to be sure, physically active. He fishes, he farms; but these are mainly expressions of his inner life; his tenderness with sheep and lambs, for example, corresponds to his tenderness for humanity in his capacity as pastor. By type he is the rural parson common in English-language literature ever since Chaucer limned his "povre persoun of a toun." Not only is Parson Tillyard a supremely spiritual man but he is a supremely good man; and this goodness makes the novelist's task all the more exacting. No character is more difficult to depict convincingly than a saintly one. Literature is replete with failures in the attempt; there have been only a few successes, notably Dostoyevsky's Prince Myshkin, Cervantes' Don Quixote, and Dickens' Barnaby Rudge. Parson Tillyard, about whom even his wife can say that he never had "a real reason to be ashamed of himself" (288), can take his place in this illustrious company. Despite his saintliness, he is convincingly alive.

The secret of Miss Chase's achievement, perhaps her most remarkable in characterization, lies in the fact that she has understood that in such transcendent goodness as John Tillyard's there is, and must be, an element of the absurd or the quixotic—as Turgenev has pointed out in his famous essay, known undoubtedly to Miss Chase, on Hamlet and Don Quixote. The entirely good character must, of course, refuse to recognize the limitations of human endeavor. If he did not so refuse, he would not persist in his life of goodness, which by very definition must express itself in good will and good works for others. And he must believe that men at heart are "generous and kind, aware of their parts in the drama of existence, able and eager to play them nobly and well" (116). This quixotic attitude is shared by all such characters in literature from the Don himself to Myshkin. Their faith in God gives them faith in people; or *vice versa;* it matters little which.

The quixotic is a strong and endearing quality in all of John Tillyard's activities and decisions: his insistence on traveling steerage, his pilgrimage to Walden Pond, and above all his entertainment in his house of patients from the State Asylum. He believes that the mentally ill will respond to the ordinary human kindnesses of a harmonious home. He is, of course, right to a certain extent. But the first two visits end in failure. Mr. Wheeler, a teacher of ancient history, who believes himself to be Julius Caesar, mounts the parson's farm horse at dawn stark naked except for a blanket over his shoulders, preparatory to a triumphal march through the streets of Rome. The second visitor, the kleptomaniac Mrs. Nesbit, returns to the hospital with a sizable portion of her host's household articles. But the third patient, Mrs. Gowan, who thinks she is Betsy Ross and more or less continuously sews flags and receives visits from General Washington, discontinues her "trips to Philadelphia" after a few visits with the Tillyards. Following Ansie's death, she relapses, but only temporarily. Mrs. Gowan is, in fact, one of the most interesting characters in the book. Part of her history—her stealing money from her bigoted Methodist mother so that she could go to Boston to marry a man, a professional thief, who had advertised in a newspaper for a wife—had been previously told in a short story, "Mrs. Gowan Gives Notice," which Miss Chase wrote for the *Atlantic* of May, 1932. The earlier Mrs. Gowan, who antedates the one in the novel by twenty-eight years, is not insane herself, though she had a job in an asylum. Both have been victims of an inhumane distortion of Christianity, but the later one, is saved by love, the essence of true Christianity.

In the Reverend Mr. Tillyard's dealings with psychopaths there is much that is fantastic, for (to repeat) perfect goodness like his is fantastic, as Miss Chase fully realizes. Had she treated these situations with solemnity, the effect would have been sentimental and no more. But she treats them with humor. Not only she and the reader but the housekeeper, Mrs. Baxter, and Mrs. Tillyard laugh at the parson's doings, which naturally no women would have put up with had they not recognized in them the inevitable expression of saintliness.

Parson Tillyard's vagary—as the world would consider it—in inviting the mentally ill to his home in fact paralleled occurrences in Miss Chase's own family. Her father, who was an overseer, or trustee, of the State Hospital at Augusta and at Bangor, was deeply concerned with the plight of the insane and invited some of them to visit in his house in Blue Hill. Thus Mrs. Gowan and the others in *The Lovely Ambition,* as well as the deranged women in *The Plum Tree,* may well be echoings from this phase of Miss Chase's experience.

The lovely ambition alluded to in the title of the novel is that celebrated in Stephen Spender's magnificent poem, "I think continually of those who were truly great," in which he praises "the names of those who in their lives fought for life. . . ." This is a Platonic poem, a Transcendental and Wordsworthian poem. It honors those human souls who have remembered their origins in places where "the hours are suns," and who find in this world traces of the eternity from which they spring. John Tillyard, quixotic though he is, is "one of those who in their lives fought for life." His favorite chore in farming in England was keeping vigil in the lambing meadow, assisting new life to be born, and ministering to it in the first precarious hours.

Never does he forget his own worth nor that of others. He knows that the human soul may be killed by ministrations not stemming from love. "Primitive Methodist" evangelism, for example, appalls him with its bludgeoning, menacing tactics. One does not scare people into permanent conversion. Rather one leads them into it by the sincerity of one's own faith, even by humor, but never by terror. And never by logic. He considers all attempts to prove God's existence to be futile and foolish. His faith is like Pascal's "wager." "He simply staked all that he had and was on a tremendous gamble that God lived and moved among us and that His active concern for His world and for all His creatures was constant, invulnerable, and unfailing" (34). His favorite Saint is Anselm, who had taught that before one could hope for an understanding of God one must believe in Him, recklessly, discarding all one's logical doubts and misgivings.

The parson's love of God opens many doors to him. It leads him to an awareness of the miraculous in the natural world—the birds, the flowers, the insects. It overflows into "a love and concern for all men, and especially for the humble and undistinguished among them" (35), and this love gives him the key to the minds of lowly people. But above all it gives him trust. Tillyard named his son Anselm; but when Anselm is taken from him, he does not lose faith.

John Tillyard's religious and philosophical convictions are extensions of those expressed in others of Miss Chase's books either by herself or by her characters. For their depth, their tolerance, their downright good sense they are worth examining. He does not, for example, believe that clergymen are "called" to their profession. He places himself solidly on the side of free will as opposed to determinism of any sort, divine or natural, in the molding of our lives. God's purposes, he thinks, "are far higher than mere plans. . . . He has given us freedom to make our own decisions as to the way we lead our lives. He means for us to choose as best we know how, and then pay whatever costs there may be from our own choices" (70). Yet God depends on us, acting freely, to work out His purposes.

Grace, the parson thinks, is not merely God's mercy or forgiveness. In fact, he is a little sick of all the Methodist talk on forgiveness, for such ideas can lead persons into religious melancholy as they did Mrs. Gowan, whose hatred and fear of her ranting Methodist mother was at the bottom of her escape into the world of Betsy Ross and General Washington. To the parson, grace is merely the presence of God, to be perceived everywhere and at all times if one will only put himself into a receptive frame of mind like that of the Tillyard family and Mrs. Gowan when they sit tranquilly talking in the parson's orchard. But John Tillyard does not advocate that we close our eyes to evil. Children should be nurtured not only on the good but also on the hard things of this world. They must learn that humanity is responsible for all the evil in the world as well as the good. Without such knowledge, their understanding is incomplete: "No one can really experience pleasure unless he knows pain as well" (168). Always, of course, one must eschew "impure, unjust, or merely selfish thought or desire," which, whether acted upon or not, holds "the power to darken untold thousands of hearts and minds, quite unknown to one another and yet mysteriously linked together" (284). Thus, since each person is involved in all, the scholar's life which Parson Tillyard leads is only superficially lonely: "Reflection and study, contemplation and worship were not, then, solitary pursuits to one who embraced them with understanding. Instead, they provided an invisible manna for the restoration and hope of one's fellow men" (284).

Such is John Tillyard's theology and philosophy, and it bears fruit for him and his family and friends. The test of any way of life is the amount of peace and unselfish joy it brings to oneself and others. The Tillyard household has these in abundance; it also has those rarer moments of an almost mystical ecstasy when life and the whole world seem entirely good and blissful and all fears and doubts drop away. It is such transfiguring moments that give existence its final meaning and answer.

All persons cannot be so fully possessed by the lovely ambition as was John Tillyard. Mrs. Tillyard, for example, loves and admires her husband but needs a sense of humor to live with him. His faith in the goodness and perfectibility of man she finds preposterous. Yet she knows that, if he believed otherwise, she and her children would not love him as they do. At the time he decides to invite the mental patients to his house, she is not sure that he is not as mad as they; but, of course, she cannot tell him so. When the first of these "experiments in hope and faith," the visit of Mr. Wheeler of the Caesar complex, proves a failure, she does not veto further experiments; in fact, it is she who invites Mrs. Gowan. She has attained a philosophy more profound, many will think, than her husband's. She simply accepts the injustice, imperfections, and impurities of life without indignation or anger against her husband for trying to remedy the incurable. Nothing can be done for Mr. Wheeler, she knows, nor for Mrs. Nesbit. But she cannot condemn her husband for trying, and perhaps some time his efforts will miraculously succeed, as they indeed do with Mrs. Gowan. Who could in fact condemn one who has made it his life's mission "to bind up the brokenhearted, to proclaim liberty to the captives, and the opening of prison to them that are bound"? (207).

CHAPTER 6

Biography: A Frontier Parson and a New York Millionairess

I Jonathan Fisher, Maine Parson, 1768-1847

IN HER TEXTBOOK for college composition courses, *Constructive Theme Writing*, first published in 1929, Mary Ellen Chase distinguishes between expository and interpretive biography. Neither kind attempts to be exhaustive. Both are selective rather than all-inclusive, their purpose being to make their subject "stand out" (422). But the expository biography displays on equal terms many traits, whether contradictory or not. The first of Miss Chase's two book-length biographies, *Jonathan Fisher, Maine Parson, 1768-1847*, published in 1948, is of the expository type.

Miss Chase's biography of Jonathan Fisher is one of her major books about Maine, taking its place beside *A Goodly Heritage, The White Gate*, and the three Maine novels. In it she presents that all-important figure in rural America of a century or two ago, the pastor whose activities, if he were worthy of his hire, extended far beyond his pulpit. Such a man set the tone of a community's spiritual, moral, cultural, educational, and political life; and Jonathan Fisher fulfilled his many functions with zeal and distinction. He became so much a part of the life of Blue Hill that his biography is essentially the history of the town in its first half-century. Miss Chase furnishes us the portrait of an extraordinary individual. Also she gives us a detailed description of a typical port town, the kind that the old shipmasters sailed away from but always returned to in the days of deep-water sailing. Elsewhere in her books on Maine seafaring, Miss Chase gives us some description of the coastal town, but she keeps the reader's eyes always on the far horizons, not exclusively on the land and its concerns, as is the case with *Jonathan Fisher*.

What manner of man was Jonathan Fisher? To begin with, he was a parson directly in the tradition of old-time Puritanism. There is not a Calvinist doctrine that he did not believe in—predestination, original sin, election, sanctification, perseverance of saints. In church polity he staunchly supported the autonomy of each congregation, and he advocated and practiced church discipline—the admonition of sinners and the requirement, on pain of excommunication, that they confess their sins before the assembled congregation. So unbending was he in doctrine that in the course of the years he lost many of his parishioners either to the less rigorous Baptist Church or, which was worse, to no church at all.

Eventually he was forced to resign. People had become bored with his insistence on election, the doctrine that holds that God at the beginning of time has chosen the souls of some for salvation, just as he has booked others for damnation, and that the efforts of the individual in doing good works have no bearing on his final consignment to heaven or to hell. But even more unpalatable to his parish had been his use of excommunication, especially during the first half of his pastorate. This most stringent of all punishments could, of course, result only in bitterness and great disunity, especially when inflicted upon prominent citizens.

In many ways Jonathan Fisher's religion was an unlovely one, the type of Calvinism of which the best one can say is that it served admirably in the hard conditions of wilderness colonization. And Blue Hill was a frontier in Jonathan Fisher's first years as pastor. In leaving Massachusetts for this distant settlement, he was throwing himself into a situation comparable to that in which his forerunners in seventeenth-century New England had labored. In fact, he chose this difficult parish intentionally, since he had had the offer of a church in an established Massachusetts town. In keeping his people in line, many of them rough and illiterate, Father Fisher, as he was called, employed the time-worn device of fear. His sermons were frequently, but by no means invariably, of the hell-fire-and-brimstone variety most notoriously exemplified by Jonathan Edwards' "Sinners in the

Hands of an Angry God," itself written for an unruly backwoods congregation.

An excerpt from one of Father Fisher's sermons will do much to explain his waning popularity when church doctrines were becoming milder all over America, even in remotest Maine. For those who have transgressed the divine law, he predicts the following unpleasantness on the day of judgment:

> You will be the subject of inward horror and burning anguish. *You cannot avoid this. There is no escaping.* [Italics are Fisher's]. You will be forced away into this place of eternal fire, prepared for the Devil and his angels. Material fire like salt will constantly penetrate and torment, but *never* decompose or annihilate your bodies. In all this you will find what it means that God is a consuming fire. . . . I desire you to understand your danger, the dreadfulness of the distress you risk. . . . Therefore it is that I bring before you the same interesting topic so frequently (118).

Like most Puritan pastors, Father Fisher could be as ruthless with himself as with his congregation. Forever examining his own soul, he was far from happy with what he found. Some of his worries seemed a bit ludicrous. He deplored his fondness for food, especially for melons, and his penchant for beaver hats. But at times his misgivings were more serious, as when he doubted the validity of his own conversion and questioned whether his writs of excommunication might apply to the shepherd as well as the sheep.

The stern, dogmatic side of Father Fisher was very real, but it was not his whole character. He was a Puritan, to be sure, but not a caricature of one, not a monstrosity. He was a man of many interests and pleasures, though the latter he attempted to disguise as duties. He was an avid reader of verse—Milton, Young, Thomson—and he even read novels. He loved to paint pictures, both in oil and water color, especially of animals, plants, and landscapes. He wrote poetry by the volume, most of it very bad; and he wrote not only theological treatises but also books for children, one of them illustrated with woodcuts. Some of his books and broadsides he sold by hawking them from house to house. He enjoyed walking, his chief means of getting around his far-flung parish and of traveling to other towns, sometimes as far as thirty-five miles away. He liked hunting and fishing, both of which frivolities he could justify as means of providing food for his family; and he took great pride in his gardening, especially in his success with the melons that tempted him so—no mean horticultural feat on the Maine coast. An ardent linguist, he studied Malay, Arabic, and Hebrew mainly for fun; he got far in the compilation of a Hebrew-English lexicon and made lists of words from the language of the Penobscot Indians. He was every bit a Yankee in his knack and pleasure in contriving mechanical gadgets, his most ambitious project being a clock with wooden works. He secretly preferred mathematics to theology, and he made considerable money as a surveyor.

Like any village minister in his day or earlier in New England, he did much physical labor. He did the carpentry and general upkeep required on the church, work for which the town paid him a dollar a day. He painted ornamental designs on sleighs, and he lettered signs and the names on the ships that were built and launched at Blue Hill. He farmed his own large parcel of land, raising most of the food required by his large household. His versatility was surely a match for that of the Maine farmer-fishermen who were his spiritual charges, and his intellectual accomplishments surpassed those of any one else in the area. Aside from being typical of the rural ministry of the times, this combining of manual and mental labor reflected the attitude of the New England intellectuals as a class. Thoreau, Emerson, even Hawthorne, and certainly Whittier in his youth, all did physical work either of necessity or for pleasure.

Parson Fisher had nine children for whom his main concern was the welfare of their souls. He was constantly fretting as to whether they had "hopes," that is, of conversion and ultimate salvation. When one of his sons lay dying, the father exhorted and examined him as to his spiritual state. A child about to die was, of course, made fully aware of his condition so that he could prepare himself for the next world. There was none of the deception and lying that surrounds the modern deathbed. If the dying child showed signs of regeneration, the parent rejoiced. Death in itself did not appall Parson Fisher; indeed, he looked on death as a desideratum for the "saved." Dying well—in a state of grace—was as important as living well. The death of anyone, whether he were among the "saints" (full communicants of the church) or an unrepentant murderer, was potentially edifying.

The Reverend Mr. Fisher attended at least two hangings, endeavoring to induce a last-minute change of heart in the condemned. About both events he wrote moralizing ballads which he illustrated with his own drawings, printed, and sold at a worth-while monetary profit to himself and, it is to be hoped, spiritual profit to his buyers.

Father Fisher was constantly busying himself in civic works. He was a major influence in the founding of the now famous Bangor Theological Seminary. Though a moderate drinker in his early years, he became a teetotaler as an example to those whose use of alcohol was injurious. He felt it wrong to enjoy what brought misery to others. He actively supported the temperance agitation that was to make Maine the first prohibition state. Convinced of the sinfulness of slavery, he nevertheless was of the opinion that emancipation alone would not solve the Negroes' problems. Until the general populace of the South—and we may now add, North—became religiously regenerate, the lot of the freed slave might be worse than that of the bondsman. Hence Father Fisher became a zealous supporter of the colonization movement which sent slaves, voluntarily freed by their masters, to settle in Africa. This expedient, he thought, would have to suffice until religion gained a firm foothold in the hearts of the Southerners.

In all the causes that he supported, Father Fisher first ascertained to his own satisfaction that he was on God's side; then he gave himself without reserve. Nor was he afraid to express his opinion on political matters. Unlike the clergy of today, he had no tender conscience concerning the divided functions of church and state. Thus he was outspoken against the War of 1812, ruinous to New England shipping; the opinions and programs of Jefferson and Jackson; and the statehood of Maine, in separation from Massachusetts.

Finally Father Fisher was very much the shrewd and practical Yankee in handling his business affairs. He did not accept the first offer made by the settlers who sought him out for their wilderness parish, but parried with terms of his own as to salary, cords of firewood to be supplied each year, and land to be allotted and cleared for him. His turning his literary ventures to profit we have already noted. In addition, he sold produce from his farm and kept his family busy making marketable products such as yarn and buttons. But his shrewdness did not carry over into his pastoral relationships, in which the truth, as he saw it, was his sole guide.

In many ways Jonathan Fisher reminds one of Cotton Mather, who in recent years has stood in many minds for all that is repulsive in Puritanism. Both combined clerical piety with scientific and literary interests and with profound scholarliness. Both mingled in political matters, and both attempted to be the supreme influence in their communities. Both were constantly engaged in works of uplift. Similarly, in his scientific and literary interests, in his proneness to rather morbid introspection, his hell-fire preaching, his perfectionism in spiritual matters, Father Fisher is reminiscent of the much, but unjustly, maligned Jonathan Edwards. But Father Fisher is more than simply a facsimile of either of these towering divines. He is more, as has been said, than simply a typical Puritan minister. Miss Chase's very great triumph in this book has been to present us such a man, not just as a dogmatist in theology and a rigorist in living but as a likable, sometimes laughable human being with a capacity for enjoying beauty and a talent for living; a man with foibles as well as greatness, weakness as well as strength. In all of American literature there is no other portrait of a Puritan clergyman at once so appealing and so convincing. If for no other reason than that it tends to soften our impressions of the Puritan clergy, who have been the butt of so much vituperation, this book is important.

To create for the present-day reader a sympathetic likeness of a man with so many traits that are unpalatable to our times is a major literary feat. To Miss Chase herself many characteristics of Parson Fisher and his religion are repugnant. She never could stomach the Calvinist's insistence on personal experience, or conversion, as necessary to full church membership even as required in her own day, much less in the intensified form of three generations earlier. The rigid adherence to doctrines such as election she also finds irrelevant to religion. Nor does she envisage God as a consuming fire—the guise in which Parson Fisher customarily saw Him. Even the physical bareness of Congregationalism—the lack of ornament and symbols in architecture and ritual—is, as we have seen, regrettable to her. And of course she cannot condone the parson's incredibly inflexible code of morality which condemned the theater and most novels, threatened a man with excommunication for betting on a horse race, and advocated discussion of religion as the fittest entertainment for a social gathering of the young. But, in spite of her rejection of so many of the standards that he himself would have gone to the stake to defend, she admires Father Fisher as a minister and has affection for him as a person.

How does she convey her admiration and love of Parson Fisher to the reader? First, she makes us acquainted with all his activities—religious, political, business, literary. The record is so impressive that we cannot help admiring the man who could do so many things, even though we are repelled by so many of his views. Second, wherever possible she shows us the pastor in lights appealing to the modern temperament, as when he preaches a sermon on God as love, instead of on God as wrath and consuming fire, and calls upon his listeners to be kind to all of God's creatures, even the ant. Or she may present him in a whimsical mood, as when he indulges his bent for mathematics to calculate for his congregation the number of redeemed there will be at the end of the millennium. With engaging optimism for a Calvinist, he assumes that two thirds of the sixty billion souls that he reckons will be judged are among the elect and will have to be assigned quarters in Paradise. Allowing one square rod for each soul, these forty billion objects of divine grace will occupy 399,414 square miles of space. The Father's house must be one of many mansions!

But Mary Ellen Chase's most effective device in humanizing her parson is irony, precisely the approach she uses with Parson Tillyard, whose quixotism Father Fisher shares to no small degree. When the going begins to be precarious, when the spectacle of Father Fisher's bigotry and mulishness threatens to disgust the reader, irony comes to the rescue. For example, by a turn of phrase Miss Chase brings a smile of tolerance and amusement to the lips of a reader who would otherwise be repelled by the parson's ghoulish interest in hangings: "The years 1811 and 1825 were immensely enlivened for Father Fisher by two hangings in which he took a prominent part in diverse ways; as spiritual adviser to the condemned, as interested onlooker, and as scribe" (189). Irony has softened to a mere human foible, which it undoubtedly was, what might otherwise be taken, or mistaken, for sheer morbid curiosity or for a willingness to profit by someone else's misfortune.

In discussing the complete lack of the spirit of compromise in Father Fisher's make-up, she brings his intransigeancy into perspective by understatement: "He did not know how to pour oil on troubled waters, nor, had he known, would his conscience have allowed him to employ so conciliatory a method" (111). Or, in commenting on the minister's avoidance in his diary of any statement the least bit sentimental and his forbidding habit of referring to his wife either as his "consort" or as Mrs. Fisher, even in letters to his children, Miss Chase writes: "Mrs. Fisher was undoubtedly a good wife, although she is seldom accorded even that companionable name" (127). Thus by irony she is able to place Jonathan Fisher's qualities that are most offensive to the twentieth century in the larger context of his whole character, which all can admire provided they can sometimes laugh at it.

Miss Chase wrote her biography of Jonathan Fisher to perpetuate the record of a life that she thought had contributed much to its day and place—a life that was at once typical and individual—just as "in his brief, yet significant and moving, biography, *John Gilley, Maine Farmer and Fisherman,* President Eliot [of Harvard] gives as a reason for his book his desire to preserve . . . the memory of a man whose dignity, honesty, and vitality and whose perception and use of life redeemed in no small way his day and generation" (xvii). The reference to Eliot's book, a classic of its sort, is significant; for it deals with a locality in Maine, Mt. Desert Island, only a few miles from Blue Hill; and, like so many of Miss Chase's works, Eliot's is a tribute to the coastal way of life and to the values it generated.

The biography of Jonathan Fisher was not easy to write. The meticulous parson left mountains of manuscript, diary and copied letters, most of them written in a code, or shorthand, of his own devising. The collecting, sorting, deciphering, and transcribing of this material and the gathering of other pertinent data were the work of many minds and hands—descendants of Father Fisher, residents of Blue Hill, relatives of Miss Chase, numerous librarians and archivists. Miss Chase describes herself as little more than a scribe, but this is an understatement. If much of the preliminary work was done by others, the writing is hers—and it is hers at its very best. Her accomplishment has been the artist's one of converting a mass of inert matter into the breathing portrait of a man, as the reviewers, among them Perry Miller and Henry Steele Commager, were quick to recognize.

II Abby Aldrich Rockefeller

Jonathan Fisher, we have seen, is what Miss Chase calls an expository biography. It presents all facets of its subject's character allowing none to become so dominant as to overshadow other traits. *Abby Aldrich Rockefeller*, the second of Miss Chase's full-length biographies and published in 1950 only two years after *Jonathan Fisher*, belongs to the interpretive category, where one set of characteristics dominates the portrait. It is surprising that Miss Chase made this choice of method since she alludes in her Preface to the vast accumulation of papers that she and her helpers combed in selecting the material for what was to be a one-hundred-and-sixty-page book. Furthermore, Mrs. Rockefeller clearly possessed the "rich and varied personality" that Mary Ellen Chase thinks is especially adapted for expository treatment. The fact that the biography was serialized in two issues of *Good Housekeeping*—June and July of 1950—accounts for its brevity and for the selectivity in the use of the material. But it is not so brief as to necessitate its rather limited presentation of Mrs. Rockefeller's character.

In her Foreword, Miss Chase describes her book as "the story of an American woman, whose generous years in terms of time were generously spent in terms of service." Even before the book begins, the biographer becomes interpretive, characterizing Mrs. Rockefeller as a woman "of wit, charm, and gaiety, . . . with a rare understanding and love of people . . . keen intelligence and quick sense of values . . . and eager awareness of what life may mean when it is regarded as a loan and not as a mere possession." She is presented as "the center and security of a large family; . . . the patron of American culture in many forms; . . . the disciple and the apostle of all things just and true, honest, lovely and of good report."

Miss Chase leaves little to the reader's judgment or imagination—a disappointment after *Jonathan Fisher*. For many this approach lessens the fun of reading. Miss Chase herself has stated that reading is a creative process in which the imagination and the mind of the reader translate the bare print into images and ideas. Each makes of a page only what his peculiar experience and talents permit. Constant interpolation and evaluation on the part of an author deprives him of the excitement of using what creative and reasoning abilities he may have.

Mrs. Rockefeller was unquestionably an exemplary wife and mother, an outstanding patron of modern and folk art, and a sincere and effective philanthropist. In presenting her as such, the biography certainly performs a useful function. Yet is it possible for one to live so long and so fully as Mrs. Rockefeller without knowing many moments of doubt or despair, or of exultant faith or ecstatic joy? Few such depths and heights are recorded in Miss Chase's book. Mrs. Rockefeller seems almost stunted emotionally. On the basis of Miss Chase's information, we know that this could not really be so. One cannot survive for seventy-five or more years, be the mother of a large family, be sensitive to the fine arts and to the suffering of humanity and not know the extremes of sorrow and of joy.

We know that Mrs. Rockefeller was sympathetically aware of the plight of immigrants and of racial minorities in New York, and that during the Depression she worried over the unemployed workers for Standard Oil of New Jersey, coming to their aid tactfully and effectively. But the biography does not give us any insight into her feelings about her own position in the economic system that necessitated her good works. Further, we are told that she was a pacifist in the 1930's before Hitler's threat to the world caused her to change her outlook. For a woman with her conservative and conventional background—she was the daughter of a United States Senator from Rhode Island—to be a pacifist at all bespeaks an intensity of spirit and of thought about history and religion that are not accounted for in the biography. And to be forced by circumstances to cease being a pacifist entails for a person of Mrs. Rockefeller's sincerity a soul-searching that again goes largely unrecorded.

How Miss Chase happened to write this book so much on a surface level is difficult to explain, especially in the light of her biographical triumph in *Jonathan Fisher* just two years earlier. One can, of course, understand her admiration for Mrs. Rockefeller, whose intelligence, self-reliance, wit, and sincere and deep religious convictions make her a model New England woman of the type Miss Chase has depicted in many of her books. But admiration for a person does not preclude analysis, nor does it explain why in this book Miss Chase's talent for irony—one of the strengths of her style—is in total abeyance. Used with grace and good humor, as Miss Chase can use it, irony was never more needed; for irony is the scalpel with which a skillful writer lays bare the truth beneath appearances.

CHAPTER 7

Aristocracy of Spirit: The Art of the Essay

MARY ELLEN CHASE'S first literary success was in fiction, and her reputation today rests, and will continue to rest, on her novels. Yet, among her own enthusiasms both as a writer and a reader, the essay takes a place second to none. The great essayists—Lamb, Hazlitt, De Quincey—first awakened her to the infinite potential of the English sentence. The grandeur and subtleties of their style, discovered, as we have already seen, during her convalescence in Montana, decided her to devote her life to the teaching—and, if possible, the writing—of great prose. Sentences that particularly thrilled her, she committed to memory, so that she could recite them on her walks or while lying in bed. Like many writers before her, she imitated her favorites: Hazlitt for his monosyllabic honesty, Pater for his skill in participles, De Quincey for his loftiness. She plunged herself into the great tradition of English prose, and the effects of that baptism are evident to the present day in the roll and the sweep and, on occasion, the conciseness of her own sentences. Like so many American authors of the past and present, she is fascinated with style, with rhetoric; but she does not permit her enchantment to betray her into bombast, as was the case sometimes with Melville and with Thomas Wolfe; or into excessive complexity, as happens on certain pages of Faulkner and Henry James. Good sense and the restraint imposed on her by her models have kept her style always well within the limits of moderation and understandability. Never does her style stand between her meaning and the reader.

Among essayists of our century, Miss Chase places Agnes Repplier at the very top. In an article entitled "The Dean of

American Essayists," written for *Commonweal,* August 18, 1933, Miss Chase lists the qualities that give Miss Repplier this eminence. Among them are humor, humane scholarship as distinguished from pedantry, irony and a sense of the dramatic, and a flare for epigrams. All of these qualities—which she believed Agnes Repplier possessed in a degree shared by no other American or English essayist of her time—combine into the most important quality of all, aristocracy of spirit. But aristocracy of spirit is something in addition; it is that quality of mind and personality that prompts one to carry one's learning lightly, to use one's talents with grace, to be aware of one's responsibility as an author, and to write with discrimination, sincerity, and honesty. The essayist need not be the discoverer of new truths, but he must be able to renew old truths, making them fresh and significant again in the reader's mind.

I The Golden Asse, and Other Essays

Between 1926 and 1928 Miss Chase wrote eight essays of high literary quality, of which four were printed in *The Atlantic Monthly,* three in *Commonweal,* and one in *The North American Review.* In 1929 these essays were gathered into a volume called *The Golden Asse, and Other Essays,* published by Henry Holt and Company. The collection consists mainly of essays of reminiscence and anecdote—recollections, somewhat in the manner of Charles Lamb, of her Maine childhood, about which she always does her best writing, and of her more recent impressions at St. Hilda's Convent, actually St. Catherine's Convent in St. Paul, where she had spent many happy days. Miss Chase clothes her commonplace subjects—a backwoods Maine herbalist, a donkey owned by her family in Blue Hill, a nun with a zeal for gardening—in garments of Biblical and Classical allusions which give them meaning by uniting them to the universal human experience. The sentences are rhythmical and varied, now periodic, now simple, like those of the great essayists; and the diction, like theirs, is concrete and image-making. In metaphor and simile, her style is not to be surpassed even by her masters.

In these essays Miss Chase brings to the fore more succinctly than anywhere else the paradox of spiritual richness and spiritual poverty in the New England of her girlhood. Individual experience, she always maintains, is made meaningful only insofar as it can be related to the deepest and best that has been thought and felt in all ages. The Classical and literary education traditional to New England, as well as the frequent and methodical exposure to the Bible in the churches, served well in this respect. To take a minor instance, the Chase children as a result of their education, both religious and secular, could think of their family donkey not only as the animal in Apuleius' story *Metamorphoses or the Golden Asse* but as the humble beast who carried Jesus into Jerusalem a week before the Crucifixion. But, aside from its emphasis on study and knowledge of the Bible, the rural New England religion offered a singularly bland fare for the imagination, as Miss Chase had already pointed out in *Mary Christmas.* This was a serious lack if one considers the pivotal place of religion in New England life at this time. In her essay "The Saints in Maine" she criticizes the Puritan concepts of duty, conscience, piety, truth as stark abstractions to be grasped and practiced without any involvement in beauty or harmony: "The Greek ideal of a barely discernible separation between the ethical and the esthetic would have been scorned among us . . ." (146). In other cultures the Saints, who received no recognition in Protestant Maine, symbolized the virtues by the beauty of their lives. Truth, Miss Chase thinks, is made most meaningful when allied with palpable beauty—the beauty of great lives like those of the Saints. Is truth, she asks, "to be apprehended only by hypothesis and syllogism? . . . To some of us it is inevitable that the truth esthetic will transcend the truth literal, that the truth poetic and artistic is more to be desired than the truth intrinsic" (147).

This need of certain minds at least for beauty as the indispensable garment of truth may account for Miss Chase's own devotion to the Episcopal Church which adopts ritual and symbol as the handmaidens of theology. That others in New England felt the same need and satisfied it in various ways and degrees is the theme of the essay "Not in Cadiz." This is the first of Mary Ellen Chase's many allusions to her grandmother's fondness for the ancient, white-walled Spanish city; and she interprets this fondness more profoundly here than in the later books (like *Mary Peters*) in which Cadiz is a symbol. To the grandmother, New England and Cadiz were two irrevocably separate worlds. In Cadiz dancing, lovers' serenades, and wine were permissible; but in New England they were completely forbidden. The grandchildren, listening to her tales of the gleaming city at the entrance to the Mediterranean, take her to task: "But dancing is wrong, Grandmother. You tell us so yourself." But the grandmother unhesitatingly answers: "It is wrong, children. There is no question about that. It is *very* wrong here—but not in Cadiz" (55).

The grandmother is willing to let the paradox stand. There is a world of duty, the Puritan world. But there is also a world of beauty, Cadiz. Her own spirit demands, and has, both. But she attempts no reconciliation between two such conflicting demands. However, the essayist and her sister Cynthia—virtually a fictional character, though suggested by Miss Chase's younger sister Edith—who is referred to frequently in the essays, do need the reconciliation; and, in seeking it, they find the Saints, not the bluenosed Calvinist Saints but the warmhearted ones of the Medieval Church. And once one has accepted beauty as the manifestation of virtue, she goes on to say, one is freed from the incessant inner strife that splits so many Calvinist souls. With Pater, one learns that "all life should be conceived as a kind of listening," and, with St. Theresa, that "the kingdom of heaven is won by a wise passiveness" (36-37). Acceptance of beauty as the counterpart of true righteousness brings to an end the fruitless struggle of body and spirit. One's prayer then becomes that of Socrates at the end of the Phaedrus: "Give me beauty in the inward soul, and may the outward and inward man be at one" (148).

Miss Chase's attachment to the Maine coast of her girlhood is, of course, deep and abiding. She loves its people, its villages, its forests, coves, inlets, and mountains, and above all its history. Had she not loved Maine so deeply, she could not have written so poetically about it. But she could not have written so well about Maine had she overlooked its spiritual failings. Some of her novels—*Mary Christmas, Windswept,* and *The Lovely Ambition*—have been attempts to confer on the Maine setting a spiritual tradition, whether Catholic or humanistically Protestant, worthy of the physical beauty of the land and the proud heritage of its people. Like Emerson, she attempted to spiritualize the old religion that had forgotten soul for formalism and abstraction. Like Emerson, she chose the path pointed out by Plato, for her Christianity is strong in the Platonic strain that can be found in the Gospels themselves. To her, beauty is the incarnation of spirit, the outward visible sign of an inward spiritual grace. Beautiful lives, the beauty of nature and art, are but the visible forms of that which is eternal and indestructible in us and in the universe. Life in itself becomes a sacrament, a unity, instead of a ceaseless conflict between irreconcilabilities. Unlike Emerson, however, Miss Chase does not deny the very existence of evil; nor does she minimize our need to struggle against evil in ourselves and in the world. But she doesn't Calvinistically equate evil with joy, or beauty, or the senses. All of these have their place in the harmony of things. To reject them categorically as bad or as suspect is to reject all chance of attaining the good life, which is one of harmony between body and soul, the material and the ideal.

II This England

All her life Miss Chase has written essays for the leading periodicals of America, the "slicks" as well as the "qualities," and they must number in the hundreds. The peak of her achievement as essayist, however, is in the volume entitled *This England*, published by Macmillan in 1936. Written in the last months of a two-year residence in Grantchester, Cambridgeshire, these essays express an attachment to England almost as profound as her attachment to Maine. They are written with a sparkle and lightness equaled only by Irving in his loving treatment of English rural life in *The Sketchbook* and in *Bracebridge Hall;* but Miss Chase's whimsy and wit, her playful allusiveness, the gentle rhythms of her sentences, are more reminiscent of her favorite Charles Lamb.

She touches on a variety of subjects, though connected, for the most part, with the country rather than the city. Her piece on the English weather surpasses in humor even Charles Dudley Warner's uproarious "How Spring Comes to New England." Her treatment of manners, English food, the English Sunday, and railway travel are done with an irony so gentle that it becomes praise, which is what it is meant to be. Thus in the first paragraphs of "An English Sunday" she writes: "The King, the Queen, the Duke and the Duchess of York and all members of the Royal Family entrusted to God, the Psalms sung with country warmth, the prayers said, the sermon preached, and the smallest choir boy aroused from his slumbers, friends and neighbors are greeted in the churchyard, healths are enquired, and the congregation slowly disperses for roast beef and port, for chicken and champagne, or for ham and boiled potatoes, steak and kidney pie, sausages and black pudding" (151). Is not the essayist disapproving? Is she not hinting that the divine services are perfunctorily, even mechanically, gone through only to be followed by the equally uninspiring ritual of the noonday meal? Of course, Miss Chase intends to convey no such censure. Her irony—which, like all irony, seems to say the opposite of what it really means—heightens the feeling that in rural England religion and daily family living blend in a sensible and salutory way.

Another group of essays are straightforward treatments of nature as found on the British Isles: "English Trees," "Twelve Ricks," "The Spring in England." In them their author's love of farming, of flowers, and of all growing things warms and vivifies each sentence. The year-long greenness of England, the variety of the scenery, and its park-like beauty evoke some of the best descriptive writing she has done. The English, she finds, are essentially a rural people. Even though the majority of them live and work in the cities, they escape as often as possible to the countryside which to them, as to Miss Chase, is the real England.

Miss Chase has elsewhere stated that in her opinion Lamb's two most beautiful essays are "Mackery End in Hertfordshire" and "Blakesmoor in Herefordshire,"[1] each of which captures the atmosphere of a locality, just as do several essays in Miss Chase's book, notably "The West Country" and "On a Bus in Somerset." Both of these essays deal with her beloved Hardy country. The high sweeping downlands of Wiltshire, the moors and narrow valleys of Devon, and the rocky, wind-tortured coasts of Cornwall clearly remind her of the rocks and mountains and lofty skies and sweeping pasture uplands of her own eastern Maine. But what gives these essays a dramatic power—an example of the dramatic flare that Miss Chase praises so in Agnes Repplier—beyond others in the volume is that in them she has been most successful in blending the people of the region—the farmers, the shepherds, the fishermen, the villagers—into a landscape which she is convinced has been a decisive shaping force in their lives. Undoubtedly her knowledge and love of Hardy made her more perceptive of the relation of the land and its people in the West Country. But she had long been interested in precisely this relationship in Maine. At any rate, in the southwest corner of England she finds a friendly, closely knit, sturdily British people living in complete harmony with their lovely varied environment. History blends into contemporary custom and speech, racial background supplies a spice of Celtic superstition and poetry, land and sky and sea produce a touch of fatalism, or acceptance, as Miss Chase would prefer to call it. The result is the quintessence of all that is English.

If there is a blemish in Miss Chase's book, it is in those few passages where irony and humor desert her and she soars to such heights of enthusiasm that her perceptions are dimmed. How, for example, would Thomas Hardy, that annalist of lives smothered by social stratification and economic handicap, feel about a statement like this: "The average Englishman is secure in the knowledge that no position is closed to excellence and distinction from whatever class it may spring"? (134). What did the class system do to the talented Jude the Obscure? Or the peasant beauty, Tess of the D'Urbervilles? Furthermore, Miss Chase's unqualified admiration for the monarchy and the aristocracy and her assumptions of the people's sentimental allegiance to both lay her open to charges of political and social naïveté. History does not record that the English kings and barons have always deserved the love of the people, and indeed the people in times past have revolted against them and at present have whittled their power to close to zero. The royal family still enjoys much non-political prestige but the aristocracy, after the prewar blunders of the Cliveden set and the recent scandals associated with the same group, has sunk lower in status than ever. Miss Chase's book, of course, antedates both these evidences of decay in the aristocracy and its influence. Yet she was writing just after the "abdication" of Edward VIII, which shook the monarchy to its foundations.

For a literary New Englander to be deeply anglophile is nothing unusual. Most of them, like Miss Chase, are of more or less English ancestry. The very name of their region brands them as offshoots of old England. Hawthorne first gave his *English Notebooks* the title *Our Old Home;* Emerson wrote glowingly of *English Traits;* Sarah Orne Jewett wrote in praise of *The Normans* from whom, by way of England, she claimed descent. Nor does this anglophilia cease at the borders of New England, as the careers of Irving, Henry James, and T. S. Eliot testify. No one but a chauvinist would object to this veneration of the "mother country." In fact, it has been intellectually wholesome to America—as well as to England. But like any emotion it can cloud one's discrimination. Happily, it has done this only occasionally with Miss Chase. *This England* remains the height of her art as an essayist, almost a perfect work in its genre.

III *A Debatable Field*

As a professor of English Mary Ellen Chase has written or collaborated in three textbooks, two of them already mentioned in other contexts: *The Art of Narration* (1926), with Frances Del Plaine, her friend at the University of Minnesota; *The Writing of Informal Essays* (1928) with Margaret Eliot Macgregor of Smith; and *Constructive Theme Writing for College Freshmen* (1929), entirely her own, which has gone through three editions, the most recent one being edited by Henry Sams of Chicago University. She has also written introductions for a college edition of *Joseph Andrews,* for the Everyman edition of *Far From the Madding Crowd,* and for the Limited Editions Club editions of the *Book of Job* and the *Book of Ruth.* In all of these introductions Miss Chase is writing about books that she loves and knows thoroughly from having taught them. In them she functions as a teacher, preparing the reader for the book he is about to read but avoiding the error—found in so many introductions—of telling him what to think.

For the past forty years Miss Chase has been a steady writer of book reviews, totaling at least one hundred and fifty; most of them have appeared in the leading magazines and newspapers—*The Atlantic Monthly,* the Boston *Transcript,* the New York *Times,* the New York *Herald Tribune,* the *Saturday Review,* the *Yale Review,* and *Commonweal.* She reviews both fiction and non-fiction. In general the non-fiction books have to do with literary subjects such as Frank O'Connor's *The Mirror in the Roadway: A Study of the Modern Novel;* Maine or New England, such as Emma Mayhew Whiting's and Henry Beetle Hough's *Whaling Wives;* and books on the Bible, such as E. W. Heaton's *Everyday Life in Old Testament Times.* Any book that she reviews is tested by exacting scholarly and artistic standards. Thus she praises Richard Cary's study of Sarah Orne Jewett for its thoroughness and its judicious arrangement of materials, but she disapproves of *Whaling Wives* for its awkward construction and dearth of material. She dwells upon the wealth and depth of Chauncey Tinker's scholarship and perception as a critic in *Essays in Retrospect,* but she expresses consternation, while still recommending the book, regarding Frank O'Connor's pronunciamentos on the modern novel—as, for example, his placing Trollope on a level with Stendhal and Tolstoy and on a peak far above Thomas Hardy! She lauds the "superb presentation" of character and situation in the stories of Nadine Gordimer, which she finds reveal far more than is visible on their surface, but she deplores "the cryptic and annoying words and images" that befuddle the reader in John Updike's *Pigeon Feathers and Other Stories,* a book which she otherwise considers a revealing and probing commentary on life.

In her review of Frank O'Connor's *The Mirror in the Roadway* Miss Chase questions whether literary criticism is not a "debatable field" for a novelist to wander in. All too frequently, she feels, the novelist is liable to bring to bear too strongly his "own experience, his own problems, his own anguish,"[2] at the cost of objectivity, though this lack may be made up for by "liveliness, understanding, and sympathy," not to be found in the work of full-time critics. In Miss Chase's reviews the objectivity of a scholar is combined with the novelist's readiness to display his enthusiasms. One reason for the liveliness of her critical writing may be that Miss Chase, or her editors, select books for which she is outstandingly qualified by experience or study to review. What happier choice, for example, could be made for a teacher and student of the Bible than Father Ronald Knox's new translation of *The Psalms?* Who could better appreciate its scholarship or evaluate the quality of its language? And who would more enjoy doing the job than the author of *The Bible for the Common Reader?* Or again, who could be better suited to review David Daiches' memoir of his childhood in Scotland, *Two Worlds: An Edinburgh Jewish Childhood,* than a fellow professor of literature who is also the author of three volumes of reminiscence? Or, for a last example, who could more appropriately review Kathryn Hulme's *The Nun's Story* than Miss Chase with her sympathetic acquaintance with nuns and convents and her concern with "the never-ending struggle of the awakened human spirit, intent on redeeming, in whatever surroundings, its loan of threescore years and ten"?[3]

CHAPTER *8*

The Bible and the Modern World

I *Ageless Ideas and Ideals*

IN HER FOREWORD to her latest book (1963) *The Prophets for the Common Reader,* Miss Chase writes: "Our civilization of today sadly needs the moral, ethical, and religious convictions cherished and uttered by those teachers and leaders of Israel nearly three thousand years ago in their own troubled times." An important incentive to her writing the book, she continues, is "the desire to bring home those convictions to my readers and to emphasize those ageless ideas and ideals of human thought and behaviour as they were taught by the prophets. . . ."

Miss Chase's most widely read and most voluminous writing on literature has been her books about the Bible—*The Bible and the Common Reader* (1944), *Life and Language in the Old Testament* (1955), *Psalms for the Common Reader* (1961), and *The Prophets for the Common Reader* (1963). In addition she has edited a collection entitled *Readings from the Bible* (1952). These volumes are exactly what their titles suggest—introductions and elucidations of the Bible for the general reader. They are combinations of textbook exposition and literary criticism. They not only present essential facts and background but interpret and evaluate; they fulfill these functions without pendantry or pontification.

To Miss Chase the Bible has always been the book of books; on it she has built her artistic and spiritual life more than on any other body of literature. Her book on the Psalms begins, "When I was a child in a small village on the coast of Maine . . ." (15). It is an appropriate beginning, for that was when her knowledge of the Bible began. In school, in church, and in the home, the Bible was read, and most commonly the readings included a selection from the Psalms. In the Chase family, when the children asked for an increase of twenty-five cents a month in their allowance, the father granted it with the stipulation that they memorize verbatim a psalm of their choice.

The best and most pleasant way really to know a work of literature is to live with it from early childhood, as Miss Chase did with the Authorized Version. That she later taught the course in the Bible as literature at Smith College was a natural sequel, though her formal training had not prepared her for it. Almost inevitable were the books that grew out of this. When she learned in the 1940's to read Hebrew under the tutorship of Edith Margaret Chrystal, an eminent student of Oriental language and theology at Cambridge University, Miss Chase found herself considered an "authority," though she vigorously denies the distinction. In 1948 she was asked by the committee working on the revision of the Standard Version, a translation of which she had always been slashingly critical, to help improve the style. Though she devoted a summer to the project, having at her own expense brought Miss Chrystal from England to help with the task, she admits failure in influencing the committee. Her only triumph was in the retention of the word *stranger* in the phrase "stranger at the gate" instead of the suggested absurdity "resident alien," which she rightly characterizes as meaningless and unpoetic.

Miss Chase's protest that she is no scholar of the Bible is, of course, unwarranted modesty. Any conscientious teacher of a course at the college level is bound to become something of an expert on his subject matter, especially if he continues teaching it for as long as Miss Chase has taught the Bible. Over the years one learns the texts almost by heart, and one studies the works of other teachers and scholars as they appear and incorporates what is important into his course and publications. Thus in 1952, after the discovery of the Dead Sea Scrolls, Miss Chase brought out a revised edition of *The Bible and the Common Reader,* modifying her earlier edition as necessitated by the new knowledge. If one adds to Miss Chase's general scholarship her command of Greek, Latin, and Hebrew, one has evidence of her indisputable competency.

Mary Ellen Chase's approach to her material, also, is the objective one of the scholar. Naturally, she is in no sense a literalist. Her own creative imagination has no difficulty in shaping from the legend, myth, and half history of much of the Bible the truths that are infinitely more important, because more universal, than mere fact. But quite aside from the spiritual truths it conveys, the Bible, as the literature of a people over a span of thirteen hundred or more years, has a life of its own—a history, an esthetic, an interrelationship among different books and periods—just as does any literature, Classical Greek, for example. An understanding of the *literary* history of the Jews, then, she considers a prerequisite for a full enjoyment and comprehension of the Bible. The findings of scholars in the past century regarding authorship and chronology in the Bible have been immense and, to some, shocking, but also of an authenticity difficult to challenge. Miss Chase takes these discoveries in her stride, presenting them as the facts which they undoubtedly are.

This open-mindedness is particularly in evidence in *The Psalms for the Common Reader,* in which she rejects the belief, as old as Christianity, that the great Hebrew prophets foresaw the coming of Jesus as the Messiah: "The real truth lies in the recognition that the prophets were in a line of religious growth and development which culminated in Jesus" (192). On the other hand, she can take sides in a controversial issue, as when she questions the assertion of some authorities that the Psalms were the hymnal of the Second Temple. She favors the view of the Psalter "as an anthology of religious poetry, prepared and published for the sake of satisfying and nourishing the minds and hearts of many people, whether in the Temple or at home, or about their business" (25). With similar objectivity she discusses the literary devices in the Psalms—those tricks of the poet that heighten reader interest—even though the fanatical or squeamishly pious might deny the presence of devices or trickery in the word of God.

In all her books on the Bible, Miss Chase, scholar though she is, has refused to write pedantically and has spared the reader the handicap of footnotes. Her purpose is not to overwhelm the reader with the weight of her learning but, as she says in the Preface to *The Psalms and the Common Reader,* "to answer questions; to explain away confusion; to suggest ways and means for more intelligent and especially for more pleasurable reading; and, perhaps above all other desires, to make old and familiar words, phrases, and lines more exciting and more real through new understanding and perception of them" (9). In other words, she is in her familiar and favorite role of teacher. Like Cynthia Wescott in her first novel, *Mary Christmas,* Miss Chase is bringing to her fellow humans the healing qualities of great literature; stripping it of many of its irrelevant incrustations; and presenting it in its truest and most simple form, in which it may the better work its curative magic.

Like any good teacher, Miss Chase does not suppress her own enthusiasm. When she intensely feels the power of a certain story or piece of poetry, she does her best to make her reader feel it with the same intensity. When she finds an opinion with which she wholeheartedly agrees, she passes on her convictions to the reader, as when she quotes John Calvin's description of the Psalms: "I may truly call this book an anatomy of all parts of the soul, for no one can feel a movement of the Spirit which is not reflected in this mirror. All the sorrows, troubles, fears, doubts, hopes, pains, perplexities, stormy outbreaks by which the hearts of men are tossed, have been depicted here to the very life" (25).

Miss Chase takes her work on the scriptures very seriously. When her publishers during World War II asked her for a book, she said she would not write a novel in a time of such suffering, but she would write a book on the Bible in the hope of directing people to this source of comfort and idealism. The result was *The Bible and The Common Reader,* the first of her books in this vein. She was disappointed that only a relatively small number of copies of the book were printed, on the plea that paper was scarce; but the same publisher was able to issue one hundred thousand copies of *Forever Amber.* To Miss Chase, authors and publishers have a responsibility to their public. Sigrid Undset in an article in the New York *Times Book Review* on the day before Christmas in 1944 described *The Bible and the Common Reader* as "a labor of love"—love of the Bible, yes, but love of mankind more. As Miss Undset points out, humanity in 1944 had reverted to savagery. The world, then and now, stands in need of the Bible, not in the evangelical sense, but because the Bible is one of the chief vehicles of the values that underlie our civilization. Sigrid Undset's remarks are applicable to all

Miss Chase's books on the Bible. The purpose is invariably that of "vindicating the old traditions in the face of the new barbarianism."

II *Life and Values in the Old Testament*

The Bible and the Common Reader, The Psalms for the Common Reader and *The Prophets for the Common Reader* are informative and pleasant exposition. In them Miss Chase presents the Bible in the light of modern scholarship. They inform and stimulate, and at times they inspire as in her profound and original analysis of the Book of Job. Yet they scarcely can be classed as creative writing, even in the realm of the essay. Further, they reveal little about their author other than that she is extremely knowledgeable in her subject. One feels that any competent Biblical scholar—endowed, of course, with comparable literary skill—would write a rather similar book. This is in no way derogatory, for the books do admirably what they intend to do. Somewhat more in the style of an essay and a bit less textbookish is the middle one of her books on the Bible, *Life and Language in the Old Testament*. From it we get a clearer idea of the roots of Miss Chase's feeling for the Old Testament and for the hardy, ancient people who produced it.

What did the Bible give to a New Englander, herself destined to be a writer? What light did the Bible, in her adult years, throw on the time and place of her own upbringing? What had the Bible given to Maine, which in turn Maine handed on to her own sons and daughters? *Life and Language in the Old Testament* provides at least indirect answers to these questions. In addition, a close study of this book serves to illustrate her approach in all her treatments of the Bible; and, above all, it demonstrates the qualities of her critical and philosophical insights.

In discussing the Old Testament, Miss Chase never forgets the fact that it is the book of her own people and of her own childhood almost as much as of the people who created it. The fierce attachment of the Hebrews for their rugged, barren homeland of Judea resembled that of the Maine-coast inhabitants for their jagged shores and rocky uplands. From such attachment grew the self-dependence, the confidence growing out of clannishness, of both peoples. Just as Willa Cather saw her Nebraska immigrants in a Virgilian light—far-travelers bringing their household gods, their civilization, to a new and savage land—Mary Ellen Chase saw New England in an Old Testament light, while Sarah Orne Jewett saw in the lives of the Maine fishermen-farmers a re-enactment of much of the life of ancient Greece, itself a land where sea and mountains mingle and rocky isles festoon the coast. This propensity to see modern life in terms of the ancient and heroic, whether Hebrew, Greek, or Roman, is consistent with the humanistic view which each author adopts. Of the three writers, Miss Chase is on the firmest ground. New England had for some generations after its founding been a determined Old Testament "theocracy." Even in Mary Ellen Chase's childhood the Bible was the ultimate source of the rules by which most rural and coastal New Englanders lived.

When Mary Ellen Chase writes of the Hebrews—"From their harsh climate and the nature of their land itself, they became vigorous, alert, watchful, self-resourceful"—there can be little doubt that she is drawing an analogy with the people she knew in her own childhood in Blue Hill. She goes on to write that, because of the necessities of life in ancient Judea, the Hebrew mind developed "a respect for the individual, his heroism, his initiative, his powers of endurance, his contribution to the common good, in short his value" (25)—a list of virtues that might have been compiled from Emerson's "Self-Reliance." In some respects, of course, the analogy breaks down. For example, "the undeveloped Hebraic attitude towards time" (34), as Mary Ellen Chase describes it—an indefiniteness that is reflected in the lack of any clear-cut system of tenses in the Hebrew language—finds no survival in any part of American life, let alone that of New England.

The analogies with New England in *Life and Language in the Old Testament* are implied rather than stated. The most important contribution of the book lies in its perceptions into the literary genius of the Old Testament authors, and the wisdom they had to offer to all lands and generations. To only a limited extent does Miss Chase employ the method, popularized by Hippolyte Taine, of "explaining" this literature in terms of the race, the place, and the times that produced it. Qualities of soul and imagination that transcend physical limitations interest her much more. She sees the Hebrews' potential of violence and proneness to fanatical hatred—offshoots of an aloofness which could plumb the depths of loneliness and despair. The anguish and the doubt of Abraham, alone on Mt. Moriah, the violence of Joab and Absalom and Achitophel, the hate of Nahum—these she cites as the examples of emotions common to all mankind, but exaggerated in the intensely alive Hebrews and displayed by their poets and prophets with the honesty and candor which themselves are major traits of the "intrinsically realistic" (57) Hebrew mind.

Most remarkable about the Hebrews, she finds, is their sense of wonder and their instinct for worship; and these traits, to which the others are but secondary, in turn stem from the consummate spiritual and bodily vitality of the people.

> They were the most *alive* people of whom history bears record, alert, responsive, and forever watchful. Nothing escaped their eyes or ears; and everything which they saw or heard revealed itself to them in terms of association and meaning. That they were also great lovers was natural and inevitable. They loved life with passion, all its familiar earthly blessings, marriage, home, children, bread, animals, birds, trees, their mountains, hills, and waste places. And this devotion to life and its wonders was doubtless increased by the absence of any belief, until very late in their history, in any conscious existence after death (61).

Wonder and worship find their highest expression in the poetry of the Prophets, the Psalms, and the Book of Job. Miss Chase takes strong issue with Matthew Arnold's famous contention in his essay on "Hebraism and Hellenism" that the Hebraic mind sacrificed imagination to conscience. Arnold's is a misreading of the Bible, though an understandable misreading. In both England and America—and here she is speaking from her childhood experience—the Puritans and their descendants had erred in their insistence that the Bible is a book that tells "us what to *do* rather than what to *be* or to *become* within our innermost selves, how to escape the anger of God rather than how to sense His greatness, or the mystery of His being, or the wonder of His works" (80).

Miss Chase's rejection of Arnold's unfavorable comparison of the Jews with the Greeks is, for the Protestant mind, a major contribution to Biblical appreciation. Three or four generations of English and American youth have been spoon-fed on the Arnold essay until its words assume a scriptural authority of themselves. The result has been to fortify the tendency in the last hundred years to depreciate the Bible as an influence less wholesome than that of our Greek heritage. But from childhood Miss Chase had cherished the Bible as the chief literary, as well as religious, influence in her life. She could not push it into second place even in relation to the Greeks, whom she highly admired also. And, as she has gone through life, the Bible has assumed only broader and broader meanings to her.

In Blue Hill the Bible was God's instructions, peremptorily given, as to what we should do and how we should worship. Yet even then, thanks to her mother, who read the Bible not only as statute but also as poetry, Mary Ellen Chase learned to love as well as to fear it. She learned then to live in the two realms in which the Bible is the great guide—the realm of the conscience and that of the imagination. When she encountered persons like the Lloyd-Jones sisters at Hillside Home School, whose lives combined conscientious conduct with exercise of the imagination and a sense of wonder, she recognized them as soul mates and her own life with them flourished. When she met persons like the Chicago finishing-school mistress whose only guide in life was a Calvinist devotion to duty, she rebelled. Her friendship and admiration for nuns were also undoubtedly due to her recognition that their lives, while ruled by religion, were not stunted by it. The Church provides more than ample scope for the imagination, the sense of wonder. Friendship, mirth, love of flowers and literature as well as love (not fear) of God are as much the life of the Catholic religious, Miss Chase finds, as is a strict adherence to conventual rule.

III *Literary Technique in the Old Testament*

As an artist, Miss Chase is of course deeply interested in the Hebrew imagination, which she accuses Arnold of so grossly underestimating. Comparing it, as does Arnold, with that of the Greeks, she comes to a very different conclusion. Both the Homeric epics and the Old Testament owe their greatness to the most fundamental of the acts of the imagination—the use of folklore, whether myth or legend, to express the essential needs and aspirations not only of a people but of all humanity. The Jacob-Joseph chapters in Genesis she compares with the *Iliad* and the *Odyssey* as epic expression, finding parallels not only in characters and themes but in the use of dreams, the exile motif, trickery, a sense of hospitality.

But in the actual telling of the Greek and Hebrew stories there are striking differences. The differences are basically those between the ballad and the epic. Like the ballads, the Hebrew narratives are notable for omission; the epics for inclusion. In illustration, Miss Chase compares the presentation of Priam's grief for Hector with the account of David's grief for Absalom. Homer is lavishly descriptive, enters into the minds of his characters Priam and Achilles, and puts lengthy speeches into their mouths. The story of David is terse and shuns detail and figurative language. It states, or perhaps understates, the bare facts, and presents David as a man of few words in contrast to the loquacious Priam. Both scenes, Miss Chase thinks, rank among the greatest in literature. The Biblical one derives its power from its silence; the epic one from its sound. Through their silences, the writers of the Old Testament "were able to evoke responses and even understandings impossible to the writers of the epics. Since the Homeric poets reveal everything, conceal nothing, they trail few invisible meanings within their thousands of beautiful phrases and intricate, detailed similes" (117).

Miss Chase, we have seen, believes that great literature makes heavy demands on the reader's imagination. Reading is creative in the truest sense of the word, just as art is. Since the Biblical writers involve the reader's imagination more fundamentally than do the epic poets, Miss Chase deems them to be the greater artists. The characters of Homer live in the palaces and on the battlefields of the ancient Mediterranean world; the imagination is not intended to disengage them from their original habitat. But the Biblical characters, disencumbered as they are of carefully described surroundings, live wherever the imagination places them. They exist in eternity, whereas the Greek heroes exist in time and place.

Like all students of the Bible since Tyndal, Miss Chase is struck by the similarity between Hebrew and the Anglo-Saxon, as distinct from the Romance, element in English. Both the Anglo-Saxon and Hebrew vocabularies abound in "direct, concise, concrete, vivid and vigorous" (143) words. In both, the nouns take on added strength because of their derivation from verbs (e.g., *spring, fight*). Both lack abstract, scientific, philosophic words. In both, sentence structure is simple, and verse is measured by accent rather than by the more complicated system of feet. The glory of the King James version arises from the translators' taking advantage of these similarities. By using wherever possible the Anglo-Saxon words, they are being most faithful to the original. According to the *Cambridge History of English Literature* Shakespeare's vocabulary approximates twenty-one thousand words, Milton's thirteen thousand and the Bible's six thousand. The six thousand words of the Bible not only are the most vivid, and hence the most poetic, but also are the ones most commonly in use among native, non-bookish speakers of English like the homogeneous population of British descent who were Miss Chase's friends and neighbors in Maine.

Miss Chase's own writing does not resemble that of the Bible so much as does, for example, Hemingway's in both diction and sentence structure. Yet her pages are full of Biblical allusions and phrases. The reader should think twice before ascribing these echoings solely to conscious effort. New England villagers, like those of Blue Hill, unconsciously used scriptural language and images. Harriet Beecher Stowe exploited this trait of speech in her Maine-coast novel *The Pearl of Orr's Island.* Thus the village spinster Roxy Toothacre expresses her resignation to her lot with the words "I made up my mind pretty early that my part in the vineyard was to have hard work and no posies." And Miss Roxy is equally ready with a Biblical allusion when she says of Master Moses, the hero of the novel, that he'll "jest have to give up his particular notions . . . and come down in the dust, like all the rest of us, when the Lord sends an east wind and withers our gourds."

Mary Ellen Chase similarly in the dialogue in her novels faithfully transcribes the scriptural echoings. But also her narrative and descriptive passages abound in Biblical similes and metaphors, which she considers to be the best in all literature. She cites scores of them in her writings on the Bible: "[Man] cometh forth like a flower and is cut down"; "My days are swifter than a weaver's shuttle.... They are passed away as the swift ships"; "My judgment was as a robe and a diadem"; "Our days upon earth are a shadow." Such figures, long before she had isolated them for illustrative purposes in her studies, had become ingrained into her thinking and expression—as they had with so many New Englanders of her generation and earlier. They occur in great profusion throughout her writing and do much to enrich it. As one reads her works, one is struck by the recurrence of certain images and phrases which have become a part of her idiom. Three in particular appear more frequently than one cares to count: the wells of Baca, as symbols of spiritual refreshment; the shadow of a great rock, as a refuge for the soul; and the words, "The lines are fallen unto me in pleasant places," to signify her own or anyone else's "goodly heritage."

CHAPTER 9

Books for Children

I *Early Efforts*

MARY ELLEN CHASE reached "the foothills of her promised land" of writing as the author of stories and articles for children. At the present time, during her retirement from teaching, she is again writing for children though not to the exclusion of adult books.

Her first published material of any kind was a story about football, "His Place on the Eleven," which Miss Chase sold to *The American Boy* in 1909. When she received a check for seventeen dollars in payment for it, she thought she had arrived as a writer. In her late twenties, while recuperating from tuberculosis in Montana, she made the decision to try her hand at a full-length book for children, modestly concluding that "serious" fiction was not for one of her youthful years and limited experience. The result was *His Birthday,* her very first volume, which was published in Boston in 1915 and for which she received fifty dollars. Only forty-eight pages in length, it sold for fifty cents a copy. Telling the story of Jesus' sixth birthday, it is sentimental in tone, but contains vivid and evocative descriptions of the Nazarene hills and skies. Today *His Birthday* is as rare as a book can be. A thorough search revealed only a single copy of it, one of those placed in the Library of Congress to secure copyright.

Miss Chase's next two novels were also for children, *The Girl From the Big Horn Country* (1916) and *Virginia of Elk Creek Valley* (1917). Reflecting the author's years in the Rocky Mountains, both recount the adventures of Virginia Hunter, the daughter of a Wyoming rancher. Like *His Birthday,* they are light but competent entertainments for the young. Their themes and conflicts derive from the age-old device of contrasting differing cultures, in this case the East and the West of the United States. In the first novel Virginia leaves Wyoming to spend a year in a girls' boarding school in New England. Her Western bluntness, her wild riding on Eastern livery horses, and her pronunciation of English shock some of her teachers and schoolmates but delight others. At least the routine of the tight little boarding school community—which Miss Chase depicts with an accuracy deriving from her own experience—is enlivened as it had never been before. In the second novel, the tables are turned when Virginia's Eastern friends visit her in Wyoming during the summer vacation.

Both novels went through several editions; writing had become at least a profitable avocation for Miss Chase, and in her first year as a graduate student at the University of Minnesota she paid most of her expenses out of income from articles written for Sunday-school journals of various denominations. By 1926, however, she had published *Mary Christmas,* her first novel for adults, which, with one exception, brought to an end her writing for children till thirty years later.

The exception is *The Silver Shell,* which Miss Chase published in 1930 with Henry Holt and dedicated to her nephews and nieces, "the proud great-grandchildren of sea-captains." Years later in the Preface to *The White Gate* Miss Chase disclosed that she had difficulty in differentiating between juvenile and adult books. *The White Gate* itself is definitely a book for adults, but an intelligent child of over twelve or fourteen could read it with delight. On the other hand, *The Silver Shell,* though it is specifically for young people, is a book that parents would enjoy reading with their children. The style is slanted to no particular age-level; in fact, at least one reviewer feared that it might be too difficult for its intended readers. The vocabulary includes words likely to puzzle and, Miss Chase doubtlessly hoped, challenge a boy or girl with access to a dictionary. The sentences are the usual rhythmic, flowing, somewhat complicated ones that Miss Chase normally composes. The result is a superbly written book, especially in its descriptions of its Maine-coast setting. Grand Père Light and Great Horned Island, where the story is laid, and the ocean that surrounds them are sketched with a vividness and sureness not present in any of Miss Chase's earlier fiction and not surpassed in her late novels.

In *The Silver Shell* Miss Chase draws from her experiences with the Maine Seacoast Mission. During several summers she served as a mission worker, visiting the remoter Maine Islands and teaching in some of the lighthouses where the children otherwise had no chance for a schooling. Elsewhere, Miss Chase has written factually of the work of the Seacoast Mission. Its director was the Reverend Alexander Macdonald, "the Grenfell of Maine," who captained the Mission boat *The Sunbeam,* on its voyages among the islands and lighthouses and up and down the lonely inlets and salt-water creeks. To the poverty-stricken and sometimes quite degenerate inhabitants of these forgotten places, *The Sunbeam* brought—and its successor of the same name still brings—not only the comforts but the necessities of religion: baptism, marriage ceremonies, funeral services. Also it brought medical aid, education, warm clothing, and food. Most important of all, perhaps, Captain Macdonald's *Sunbeam* brought contact with the larger world, renewing the knowledge among isolated people that they were social beings, part of a state, a nation, and all humanity. Quite literally the *Sunbeam* brought contact with the outer world when in the winter and spring her sturdy oaken hull served as an icebreaker in opening harbors and channels.[1]

In her work for the Mission and in her acquaintance with the people whom it served Miss Chase struck a rich vein for children's fiction. Islands and lighthouses are, of course, irresistible. So is an island child like Judith, the daughter of an impoverished fisherman who discovers from reading a packet of old letters that her great-great-grandmother had been presented to the King and Queen of Spain in Cadiz a hundred years ago; or a boy like Duncan, whose one purpose in life is to follow in the footsteps of his father and grandfather as keeper of Grand Père Light; or the island idiot, Foolish Tom, who lives alone in a shack by the seaside, with only a pet bluejay for company, but who loves all life and possesses seemingly clairvoyant powers.

Many of the themes for Miss Chase's novels for adults are present in *The Silver Shell.* The vision of Cadiz, the gleaming city, so ubiquitous in her writings, serves its usual function as a talisman of release from the confinement of harsh New England reality. The silver shell itself, after which the book is named, is an agent—like the "Red Book" in *Dawn in Lyonesse*, the Irish fairy tales in *Uplands*, or Jan Pisek's or Mary Christmas' stories—in awakening the child's imagination to beauty. Judith finds the silver shell, which is beautiful beyond any shells of the North Atlantic, embedded in a cleft in a log that had drifted to the shingle beach of Great Horned Island from some far-off sun-drenched sea. It has made its far journey as a messenger from another realm, corresponding to that of the spirit, in which loveliness of form and color has its origin. Foolish Tom, who helps Judith pry loose the shell from its place of imprisonment, predicts that other great discoveries and revelations of beauty will follow. The prediction is correct; Judith proceeds from one illumination to another—the reading of her great-great-grandmother's letters, which bring her closer to the faraway place and time from which the shell drifted; a stay on Grand Père cliffs where a visiting schoolteacher leads her into the kingdom of the mind; the promise of further epiphanies in the city where the same schoolteacher is to take her to continue her education. Judith has learned well the lesson of the ancient philosopher of whom her teacher tells her: the discovery of one object of beauty, if the finder sufficiently cherishes it, leads to the discovery of countless others until one is brought face to face with eternal Beauty itself.

One incident in *The Silver Shell* brings to mind Sarah Orne Jewett's short story "The White Heron," in which a young girl climbs to the top of a towering white pine and there gets a glimpse of the rare and beautiful bird for a specimen of which an ornithologist had offered her a large reward. Judith too climbs to the dizzying height of a pine tree and views the remote outer world as far as the misty blue line of mainland hills. Though her purpose is not to behold the flight of an almost extinct white heron but rather to raise a flag to be seen by her playmates at faraway Grand Père Light, her climb too is an ascent into the purity and inviolability of the spirit where one has visions denied to dwellers on the flatness of the earth. Judith's signal is answered, as all such signals must be, not only from the lighthouse, but from even farther shores; for shortly after her descent from the tree she finds the silver shell flung up on the cobbles of Great Horned Island from God knows what distant atoll.

II *Recent Books for Children*

In 1958 Houghton Mifflin published Mary Ellen Chase's *Sailing the Seven Seas* in its North Star series for children. This book was quickly followed by *Donald McKay and the Clipper Ships* (1959) and *The Fishing Fleets of New England* (1961). All three are historically accurate, simply but not condescendingly written, and copiously and tastefully illustrated. They are in the best tradition of American juvenile writing—a tradition which has drawn upon the talents of Irving, Longfellow, Hawthorne, Jewett, and Mark Twain, and which for several generations had as its chief organ that finest of all children's magazines, *St. Nicholas.* Not many of our best authors write juveniles anymore, which is the loss of American children. That Miss Chase has revived the tradition is their gain. And, like the best books for young people in the past, Miss Chase's latest ones can be enjoyed by grown-ups as well, the ultimate test of good juvenile writing.

Of the three North Star books *Sailing the Seven Seas* deals with material already wholly familiar to Miss Chase's older readers—the prowess of the American deep-water sailors of the last century, especially those in the Far Eastern Trade. In *The Fishing Fleets of New England* she displays an equally detailed knowledge of the history of fishing and the types of ships and gear used at various periods. She is at pains to show the antiquity of the New England fisheries, which probably antedate Columbus' voyage; and she emphasizes the importance of Maine in the industry throughout the centuries. She gives proper credit to the Portuguese, Irish, and others who worked side by side with the New Englanders in making fishing a major factor in American economic development, especially in its influence in encouraging the great sailing tradition that in the nineteenth century gave the United States merchant marine a place second to none in the world. She praises the character traits of the fishermen: their skill, their courage, their endurance and energy, and their genuine religious feeling stemming from their rigid New England Protestant training or from their Old World Catholicism and strengthened by the vastness, unpredictability, and dangers of the sea on which they toil. In their lives, as in those of so many of Miss Chase's fictional characters, the awe inspired by "great waters" is a force that strikes to the depths of the spirit. Above all, she tries to convey a respect for the independence of these men—a trait which from the earliest times to the present has caused them to take their pay according to what they catch, not as an hourly wage. The old system where each man was reimbursed for what he caught "on his own hook" (this is the origin of the idiom) has been modified to a split in proceeds of a trip on a ratio of sixty per cent for the crew and forty per cent for the owners of the vessel. The incentive of working for oneself is still there and is sanctioned by the unions.

Donald McKay and the Clipper Ships is a paean to the clipper ship, which Miss Chase considers a work of idealism and art. McKay was an artist who, like all artists, was never satisfied, but always felt he could do better. As a motto for the book and again as a closing sentence Miss Chase quotes McKay's remark, "I never yet built a vessel that came up to my own ideal. I saw something in each ship which I desired to improve upon." Miss Chase, of course, revels in her subject, which is at the heart of her interest in maritime history. For her there is poetry in the life of McKay, in the times and enterprises which he represents, and in his superb creations with their stirring names—names which sum up an era: *The Flying Cloud, The Sovereign of the Seas, The Great Republic, Romance of the Seas.*

CHAPTER 10

Conclusions

WHAT IS MARY ELLEN CHASE'S ultimate place in the life of the mind and the spirit of America? Which, of her more than thirty books, have made a substantial contribution to the present, and which have a chance of continuing influential in the future?

There are several certainties. The books on the Bible have reached many, many thousands, both students and general readers, whose understanding and enjoyment of the Scriptures have been enhanced by them. There is nothing of the Gideon in Miss Chase. Her purpose is not to make religious converts. But she does consider the Bible a superlatively important body of literature, rich in beauty and philosophy. Assuredly she has helped to make these riches accessible to modern readers, whose viewpoints are often blurred either by scientific irrelevancies or by a revolt against traditional orthodoxy. A competently given course in any literature, not only in the Bible, must of necessity add to the insights of the students. This is precisely what Miss Chase has done both for the Smith girls in her classes and for whoever reads the books which are the outgrowths of these classes. The time will come when Miss Chase's books on the Bible will be out-of-date and others will supplant them. But that will be some decades from now, considering that *The Prophets for the Common Reader* appeared only in 1963. In the meanwhile, she will continue to be a humane guide to the reader who wishes to acquaint himself with the basic writings of the Jewish and Christian religions. Here is a definite contribution to our culture—tangible and undeniable.

Miss Chase's books on her Maine childhood will perhaps be longer-lived than her Biblical commentaries, for they are more personal in their subject matter and hence not likely to be displaced. Reminiscences of childhood and youth in rural and small-town America have been an important segment of our literature. Garland's *Son of the Middle Border,* Howells' *A Boy's Town,* Mark Twain's *Life on the Mississippi,* to name a few, are still read with delight. *A Goodly Heritage,* much of *A Goodly Fellowship,* and *The White Gate* are by every test among the best of American reminiscences. For a thorough presentation of the details and atmosphere of life in a small New England town, which is also typical of America just before the present century, no book has approached *A Goodly Heritage.* For the probing of a child's psychological relationship to family, neighbor, and countryside in such a town *The White Gate* is unique. Thomas Bailey Aldrich's charming recollections of boyhood in Portsmouth, New Hampshire, in *The Story of a Bad Boy,* is, for example, superficial in comparison.

Similar claims of durability can be made for the novels about Maine—*Mary Peters, Silas Crockett, The Edge of Darkness*—and with them the splendid biography of Jonathan Fisher. The very extensive literature of the New England seaboard has produced nothing comparable to them—Sarah Orne Jewett's works not excepted. In these four books is given the whole life—the settlement, the rise, the decline—of the coast from 1760 to 1950. Stylistically they are lyrical evocations of the places and times of their setting. On their pages walk a score of Peterses, Crocketts, Winships, and Holts, as well as secondary figures, all of whom, though typical of their time and place, live as individuals. Only in the absence of the eccentrics who abound in villages such as Miss Chase writes of do we feel a lack. Only in the depiction of such persons must Miss Chase take second place to Sarah Orne Jewett.

Novels that rest firmly on a foundation of social history, as do Miss Chase's Maine novels, have an advantage in retaining readership. Students or casual readers interested in Maine, New England, or maritime America will turn to Miss Chase's novels for a long time to come, just as they will turn to her autobiographical writing. The fact that they will be reading literature as well as social history may be of secondary concern to them.

Those of Miss Chase's novels which do not deal primarily with Maine life and history cannot, of course, depend on their informational value as an aid to survival. This lack may tell against them, but it is far from decisive. The two first novels *Mary Christmas* and *Uplands* are already well on the road to oblivion. But *Dawn in Lyonesse, Windswept,* and *The Lovely Ambition* are of an artistic substance that still commands respect and attention. Partly their quality stems from skill in plotting, the lyrical evocation of setting and atmosphere, the creation of memorable characters like Jan Pisek, Susan and Parson Tillyard, and Mrs. Gowan. But more important is the wholeness of view-point that informs these novels, as indeed it does all of her many books and hundreds of periodical articles. Throughout her work as writer and teacher, Miss Chase brings to bear a set of values or principles that rest on the conviction that mind and spirit supersede matter, render man unique on earth, and make him the ultimate master of his destiny.

Elsewhere in this study I have used the term *Humanism* in describing Miss Chase's insistence on the transcendency of spirit and intellect—Humanism as conceived by Irving Babbitt and Paul Elmer More and as reflected in the works of such writers as Ellen Glasgow, Willa Cather, and Robert Frost. But the tenets of Humanism are older than Plato, are basic in Judeao-Christianity, and are certainly inherent in the near deification of man in American Transcendentalism. And Humanism is the norm in American fiction in the nineteenth century. Christopher Newman in Henry James's *The American,* Silas Lapham in Howells' novel, Hester Prynne in *The Scarlet Letter*—to name only three examples—exhibit a freedom of will which disengages their lives from the meshes of environment and biochemical determinants. They are moral beings in that they have the power of choice between good and evil actions—a power which liberates them from the prison of matter.

If the will counts for nothing in human life, man's stature diminishes; he loses dignity, for he is in no way different from the rest of the material universe. But Miss Chase has undeviatingly insisted on man's self-determining potential. She rejects all theories that tend to strip man of his responsibility for his own deeds, including the theological doctrines of election and of the vocation of the clergy by divine will. In doing this, she clings stubbornly to traditions having their roots in the Old Testament and enduring, despite certain deterministic teachings of Augustine and Calvin, until the middle of the nineteenth century. Man is capable of discriminating between right and wrong and is at liberty to will his actions accordingly: this is the burden of the Bible by most present-day interpretations, of even the most fatalistic Greeks after Homer (Oedipus is destroyed not so much by the fate over which he had no control but by his arrogance, over which he does have control), and of most great literature ever since.

In the world of Miss Chase's fiction, man, of course, does not have complete mastery of his environment. He is subject to natural law; he grows old, becomes ill, dies. His plans are shattered, and his life is cut short by acts of nature; he is constantly vulnerable to accident. But the manner in which he meets the contingencies of human existence is subject to choice or will. He may resign himself to circumstances and submit to being a pawn, to being crushed. Or he may accept them as inevitable, yet not the final determining force in the quality of his life. The quality of one's living is, indeed, all-important. One may live on the material level and live a slave. Or one may live on the spiritual level where vicissitude does not penetrate.

Once one is born again in spirit, to use Miss Chase's phrase, one begins to live religiously, whether in the cloisters, the schoolroom, the artist's studio, or the factory. It would be wrong to say that Miss Chase considers religion an aid to achieving the life of the spirit. Such life is religion; the two are one.

Miss Chase's view of life may seem conservative and orthodox to many; but, beyond the fact that she expresses herself in traditional terms of Judeao-Christianity and places her stories within the framework of that tradition, she is not conservative at all. Many writers of our century are, to be sure, more Naturalistic than she: Steinbeck, Dos Passos, Dreiser. But others diverge sharply from Naturalism. Willa Cather and Ellen Glasgow are, of course, entirely Humanistic. In the work of Hemingway, who is much less obviously Humanistic, the reiterated theme of "the undefeated" is an assertion of the spirit's ascendency over circumstance. William Faulkner not only repudiated in his Nobel Prize speech the Naturalistic concepts of life (for example, the glandular determination of character) and stated his faith in man's immortality but he informs his novels with the same beliefs. Dilsey in *The Sound and the Fury* endures not as a mere physical organism but as spiritual force and does so within the context of her own Protestant Christianity. The boy in *The Bear* learns that it is not one's success or failure in hunting that is important, but the way one hunts, the quality of one's hunting. One may hunt or live with vindictiveness, recklessness, cruelty; or one may hunt, or live, with generosity, steadfastness, and compassion. It is a man's task to choose and nurture the quality of his life.

Despite her Humanism, Miss Chase is not excessively optimistic about the future of civilization. Man too infrequently lives up to his almost limitless spiritual potential in his daily existence. Philip Marston in *Windswept* wonders what will become of a world motivated by fear, hate, and greed. Parson Tillyard in *The Lovely Ambition* sounds a grave warning to America lest she lose her particular vision of freedom. The Hedonism of present-day Western life is a matter of great concern to Miss Chase. Once, she says, she considered self-pity and indifference to be the cardinal sins; now she gives first place to ease, the very hallmark of our culture.

Neither is Miss Chase excessively pessimistic; pessimism, like fatalism, is too easy a way out. Rather, she is a "desperate" optimist, to use the phrase with which her fellow Maine writer, E. A. Robinson, described himself. Like Robinson, as he states his views in "The Man Against the Sky," she rejects both the easy affirmations and the easy negations. She clings to the "orient word" and she refuses to lose sight of the "gleam," no matter how distant and blurred it may be.

Like E. A. Robinson, too, Miss Chase has stuck closely to the traditional or conventional literary forms. Three of her major novels—*Mary Peters, Silas Crockett,* and *Windswept*—are family chronicles covering from four to two generations. Here she is following a pattern established by Thomas Mann, John Galsworthy, and Sigrid Undset. Such novels are built on characterization, episode, and setting rather than on elaborate or experimental form. They are unified by recurrent symbols, or leitmotivs, like the family portraits in *Silas Crockett* or the vision of Cadiz in *Mary Peters;* or by the continuity of family traits and aspirations, as in *Silas Crockett* or *Windswept;* or by a cyclical movement, as in *Mary Peters* where the full circle of the heroine's life is indicated by the names of the four sections—"The Sea," "The

Village," "The Land," and finally "The Sea" again—each corresponding to a stage in Mary's spiritual orientation from childhood through adolescence and womanhood to old age.

Miss Chase's other novels are also conventional in form. *The Lovely Ambition* with some of the characteristics of a family chronicle is basically linear and uncomplicated in plot, as are *Mary Christmas* and *Uplands. Dawn in Lyonesse* and *The Plum Tree,* both of which were made into plays, are dramatically compact: each focuses on only one important character, and each covers only a few days of time, the action being apportioned among a limited number of rather intense scenes. Only *The Edge of Darkness* presents structural innovation. It is unique in its drastically limited time span and in its encompassing of eight or nine life stories like spokes radiating from the personality of the single strong character already dead as the novel opens.

Ultimately, literary form and style have their origins deep within an author's individuality. They are expressions of his heritage, his background, above all of his habits of thought. In short, they are expressions of the quality of his life. Among the people of Maine, as they appear in books and in real life, are many who during their years on the land, on the coast, or on the sea have been moved to think long and deeply and who are willing to share their reflections in delightful conversation with any one ready for an interchange of ideas. Throughout history, wisdom has had its origin in such interchanges, which are the flowering of a high civilization. Leisurely thoughtful talk, which is by no means dead in America, is a heritage from late Colonial times and the first fifty years of the Republic, when discussions of religion and politics flourished among all classes. Every man was to a certain extent his own philosopher and theologian and was less hesitant to express even unconventional views than he would be in our day when mass taboos are inculcated and perpetuated by mass media unheard of two generations ago. In Maine in Miss Chase's youth and, I believe, down to the present day, the inroads against independence of thought have not been so great, perhaps because of the state's position off the most congested thoroughfares of the national life. Something of the flavor of the essays of Emerson and Thoreau persist in Maine thought and talk, and level of education has surprisingly little to do with it.

Miss Chase is preeminently a Maine woman in that this flare for thoughtful, often ironical, incisive, but not unduly excited conversation is basic to her talents. An obvious expression of it is her lecturing both to general and to academic audiences, as is her highly provocative classroom teaching. But literature in its many variations rests on an oral tradition. The essay, at which Miss Chase excels, is written conversation. The novel is but a form of storytelling. Good storytellers reveal their thoughts and convictions, their observations on life. They are the most sophisticated of all conversationalists. In her novels, on which her literary reputation must rest, Mary Ellen Chase has commented on life in the accents of nineteenth-century New England—a most appropriate idiom for one writing in the mainstream of the American tradition, for one whose often stated conviction is that of the psalmist:

> The lines are fallen unto me in pleasant places;
> Yea, I have a goodly heritage.

Notes and References

Chapter One

Much of the material for this chapter has come from Mary Ellen Chase's own autobiographical writings *A Goodly Heritage* (New York, 1932), *A Goodly Fellowship* (New York, 1939), and *The White Gate* (New York, 1954). Further information has been drawn from the many autobiographical essays Miss Chase has published in periodicals, especially those essays reprinted in *The Golden Asse, and Other Essays* (New York, 1929). Many points regarding Miss Chase's life and views have been elucidated through correspondence and conversation with her.

1. Mary Ellen Chase, "Mary Ellen Chase" (part of a symposium of authors writing on their own lives), New York *Herald-Tribune Book Review* (October 24, 1954), p. 8.
2. *A Goodly Heritage*, pp. 27-28.
3. See *A Goodly Heritage*, p. 151. P. H. Boynton in *America in Contemporary Fiction* (Chicago, 1940) complains (p. 34) that Miss Chase has overlooked vestigial Puritanism in her fiction. In the pages that follow, ample evidence is given that from her earliest short story to her most recent novel she has demonstrated an acute and at times pained awareness of the Puritanism lingering in Blue Hill. Her biography, *Jonathan Fisher, Maine Parson, 1768-1847* (New York, 1948) is one of the most discerning books ever written on the Puritan outlook.
4. Henry Ward Beecher, *Norwood; or Village Life in New England* (New York, 1868), p. 2.
5. Mary Ellen Chase, "My Novels About Maine," *Colby Library Quarterly* (March, 1962), p. 16.
6. *Ibid.*, p. 15.
7. Sarah Orne Jewett, *Deephaven* (Boston, 1877), pp. 6-7.
8. New York *Herald-Tribune Book Review* (October 24, 1954), p. 8.
9. "My Novels About Maine," p. 16.

Chapter Two

A Goodly Heritage is of course the chief source of Miss Chase's views on education and for the facts of her own teaching career. Many of her numerous articles on education listed in the bibliography in this volume have supplied additional information. Especially illuminating are "Head and Hands Working Together," *Common Ground,* I (Autumn, 1940), 3-6; "An Ancient Democracy to a Modern," *Common Ground,* III (Winter, 1943), 65-71 (Miss Chase served as an advisory editor for *Common Ground* during its brief lifetime); "Progressive Education," New York *Times Magazine* (February 9, 1941), p. 11; and "The Teaching of English," in R. M. Gay (editor), *Essays on the Teaching of English* (Cambridge, Massachusetts, 1940).

1. In Eric Larrabee (editor), *American Panorama* (New York, 1957), p. 65.
2. *The Golden Asse, and Other Essays,* p. 64.

Chapter Three

1. P. H. Boynton, *America in Contemporary Fiction,* p. 33.
2. [Richard Cary], "Editor's Epilogue," *Colby Library Quarterly* (March, 1962), p. 46.
3. "Marigolds," *Harper's,* CXXXVIII (May, 1919), 825.
4. *The Bible and the Common Reader* (First Edition), p. 194.

Chapter Four

1. "My Novels About Maine," *Colby Library Quarterly* (March, 1962), p. 18.
2. *Ibid.,* p. 17.
3. *Ibid.,* p. 18.
4. *Ibid.,* p. 18.
5. *Ibid.,* p. 15.
6. *Ibid.,* p. 20.

Chapter Seven

1. "The Influence of the King James Bible on Two Great Masters of Nineteenth-Century Prose," in M. B. Crook, ed., *The Bible and Its Literary Associations* (Nashville, 1937), pp. 364-65.
2. "Frank O'Connor Subjects the Novel to Shock Treatment," a review of O'Connor's *The Mirror in the Road,* New York *Herald-Tribune Book Review* (October 7, 1956), p. 3. The review of C. B. Tinker, *Essays in Retrospect* may be found in the New York *Times Book Review* (April 25, 1948), p. 6; of Whiting's and Hough's *Whaling Wives,* in the New York *Herald-Tribune Book Review* (January 11, 1953), p. 5; of E. W. Heaton's *Everyday Life in Old*

Testament Times, in the New York *Times Book Review* (September 30, 1956), p. 5; of John Updike's *Pigeon Feathers and Other Stories,* in the New York *Herald-Tribune Book Review* (March 18, 1962), p. 4; of Richard Cary's *Sarah Orne Jewett,* in *The Colby Alumnus* (Fall, 1962) pp. 6-7; of Nadine Gordimer's *Friday's Footprint,* in the New York *Herald-Tribune Book Review* (January 10, 1960), p. 1.

3. "An Enthralling Narrative of a Profound Experience," a review of Kathryn Hulme's *The Nun's Story,* the New York *Herald-Tribune Book Review* (September 9, 1956), p. 1. The review of David Daiches' *Two Worlds* may be found in the New York *Herald-Tribune Book Review* (March 25, 1956), p. 1; of Father Ronald Knox's *The Psalms: A New Translation,* in the New York *Times Book Review* (June 15, 1947), p. 26.

Chapter Nine

1. "How Four Girls 'Discovered' Maine," *Ladies' Home Journal,* XXXIV (May, 1917), 18; "The Islands Lose a Friend," *Outlook* CXXXIII (February 21, 1928), 365-66.

Selected Bibliography

The following bibliography lists all of Mary Ellen Chase's published books and, to the best of my knowledge, all of her magazine fiction for adults. From her multitudinous articles, introductions, and contributions to books written in part by others I have selected those items that illuminate importantly her life and ideals. A large mass of writing for juvenile periodicals, much of it anonymous, remains unlocated; for Miss Chase has kept no record of her publications at any stage in her career. Of her book reviews perhaps one hundred and fifty are locatable. In the notes to Chapter VII several of these are cited, but I have included none in the Bibliography, since space is limited and Miss Chase's critical writing is more substantially represented in her books and essays.

PRIMARY SOURCES

1. *Books*

His Birthday. Boston: Pilgrim Press, 1915.

The Girl From the Big Horn Country. Boston: Page Co., 1916.

Virginia of Elk Creek Valley. Boston: Page Co., 1917.

The Art of Narration (with Frances K. Del Plaine). New York: F. S. Crofts & Co., 1926.

Mary Christmas. Boston: Little, Brown & Co., 1926.

Thomas Hardy from Serial to Novel. Minneapolis: University of Minnesota Press, 1927.

Uplands. Boston: Little Brown & Co., 1927.

The Writing of Informal Essays (with Margaret Eliot Macgregor). New York: H. Holt & Co., 1928.

The Golden Asse, and Other Essays. New York: H. Holt & Co., 1929.

Constructive Theme Writing for College Freshmen. New York: H. Holt & Co., 1929.

The Silver Shell. New York: H. Holt & Co., 1930.

A Goodly Heritage. New York: H. Holt & Co., 1932. (New edition, 1957. Reprinted by Avon Books, New York, 1945. Translated into German, 1948; into Vietnamese and Urdu, 1953; into Tamil, 1954; into Telugu and Bengali, 1955.)

Mary Peters. New York: Macmillan, 1934. (Translated into German in Vienna, 1946, and in Augsburg, 1948; into Burmese, 1956; into Hindi and Marathi, 1958.)

Silas Crockett. New York: Macmillan, 1935.

This England. New York: Macmillan, 1936. (As *In England Now* by Collins, London, 1937.)

Dawn in Lyonesse. New York: Macmillan, 1938. (By Collins, London, 1938. Adapted as a play in three acts, *Land's End,* by Thomas Job, and presented at the Playhouse, New York City, December 11, 1946.)

A Goodly Fellowship. New York: Macmillan, 1939. (By Collins, London, 1940. Translated into German, 1948. Reprinted by Bantam Books, New York, 1957. Reissued as a Macmillan paperback, 1960.)

Windswept. New York: Macmillan, 1941. (By Collins, London, 1942. Overseas Edition, Council on Books in Wartime, 1943. Translated into German, 1943; into Swedish, 1946.)

The Bible and the Common Reader. New York: Macmillan, 1944. (Revised edition, 1952. By Collins, London, 1946. Translated into German, 1951.)

Jonathan Fisher, Maine Parson, 1768-1847. New York: Macmillan, 1948.

The Plum Tree. New York: Macmillan, 1949. (By Collins, London, 1950. Edition in Braille, London, 1953. Adapted as a play by L. McMahon and R. Sengel, Dramatic Publ. Co., New York, 1953.)

Abby Aldrich Rockefeller. New York: Macmillan, 1950.

Readings From the Bible. New York, Macmillan, 1952.

Recipe For a Magic Childhood. New York: Macmillan, 1952.

The White Gate. New York: W. W. Norton & Co., 1954. (As *Adventures in the Imagination of a Child* by Collins, London, 1955. Translated into German and Sinhalese, 1958.)

Life and Language in the Old Testament. New York: W. W. Norton & Co., 1955. (By Collins, London, 1956. Translated into German, 1957.)

The Edge of Darkness. New York: W. W. Norton & Co., 1957. (By Collins, London, 1958; People's Book Club, Family Book Club, and Abridged Books, 1958. Translated into Marathi, 1959; into Persian, 1961.)

Sailing the Seven Seas. Boston: Houghton, Mifflin Co., 1958.

Donald McKay and the Clipper Ships. Boston: Houghton, Mifflin Co., 1959.

The Lovely Ambition. New York: W. W. Norton & Co., 1960. (By Collins, London, 1961. Translated into French, Spanish, Italian, German, Portuguese, Swedish, and Japanese by U.S. Information Agency, 1960; into German, Munich, 1961. In *Reader's Digest Condensed Books,* 1960. In the Philadelphia *Sunday Bulletin,* July 16 and 23, 1960.)

The Fishing Fleets of New England. Boston: Houghton, Mifflin Co., 1961.
The Psalms for the Common Reader. New York: W. W. Norton Co., 1962.
The Prophets for the Common Reader. New York: W. W. Norton Co., 1963.
Victoria: A Pig in a Pram. New York: W. W. Norton Co., 1963.

2. *Contributions to Books*

"The Influence of the King James Bible on Two Great Masters of 19th Century Prose," in M. B. Crook, ed., *The Bible and Its Literary Associations.* Nashville: Abingdon Press, 1937.
"The Teaching of English," in R. M. Gay, ed., *Essays on the Teaching of English.* Cambridge: Harvard University Press, 1940.
Preface to *The Book of Job.* New York: Limited Editions Club, 1946.
"New England: Land of God," in *Look at the U.S.A.* Boston: Houghton, Mifflin Co., 1947.
Preface to *The Book of Ruth.* New York: Limited Editions Club, 1948.
Introduction to Thomas Hardy, *Far From the Madding Crowd.* New York: Dutton, 1951. Everyman's Library edition.
"Our Goodly Heritage," in *The Northampton Book,* edited by The Tercentenary Committee. Northampton, Mass., 1954.
"On Teaching and Teachers," in D. Louise Sharp (editor), *Why Teach?* New York: H. Holt & Co., 1957.
Introduction to Henry Fielding, *Joseph Andrews.* New York: W. W. Norton & Co., 1958. The Norton Library edition.

3. *Short Stories for Adults*

"A Return to Constancy," *Harper's,* CXXXVII (November, 1918), 846-55. Reprinted in *Woman's Day* (May, 1942).
"Marigolds," *Harper's,* CXXXVIII (May, 1919), 819-25. Reprinted in *Woman's Day* (August, 1943), 24.
"Sure Dwellings," *Harper's,* CXXXIX (November, 1919), 869-76. Reprinted in *Woman's Day* (June, 1944), 22.
"Upland Pastures," *Atlantic Monthly,* CXXIX (May, 1922), 651-58.
"The Garment of Praise," *Scribner's,* LXXVIII (October, 1925), 422-32. Translated as "Le Manteau de Louange," in *La Nouvelle Semaine Artistique et Littéraire* (March 31 and April 7, 1928).
"Salesmanship," *Pictorial Review,* XXXI (July, 1930), 9. Reprinted in *Scholastic* (April 17, 1937).
"Mrs. Gowan Gives Notice," *Atlantic Monthly,* CXLIX (May, 1932), 611-19.

"Mrs. Penlust on the Damascus Road," *Atlantic Monthly,* CL (October, 1932), 411-17.
"A Pinch of Snuff," *North American Review,* CCXL (June, 1935), 122-43. Reprinted in *Woman's Day* (February, 1943), 18.
"Taxi Driver 63," *Delineator,* CXXVIII (February, 1936), 12.
"The Golden Age," *North American Review,* CCXLI (March, 1936), 135-47.
"A Candle at Night," *Collier's,* CIX (May 9, 1942), 17.
"Honeymoon, 1854," *Woman's Day* (June, 1954), p. 38.

4. *Articles in Periodicals and Newspapers*

"How Four Girls 'Discovered' Maine," *Ladies' Home Journal,* XXXIV (May, 1917), 18.
"The Islands Lose a Friend," *Outlook,* CXXXIII (February 21, 1923), 365-66.
"A Kitchen Parnassus," *Atlantic Monthly,* CXXXVIII (August, 1926), 249-54.
"The Golden Asse—A Tribute," *Atlantic Monthly,* CXXXIX (February, 1927), 212-20.
"The Saints in Maine," *Commonweal* (May 25, 1927), 64-66.
"Mystical Mathematicks," *Commonweal* (January 25, 1928), 981f.
"Not in Cadiz," *North American Review,* CCXXV (May, 1928), 606-15.
"Wormwood—For Thoughts," *Atlantic Monthly,* CXLI (May, 1928), 629-37.
"Have You Martin Chuzzlewit?" *Atlantic Monthly,* CXLII (September, 1928), 423-25.
"On Kitchens and Cloisters," *Commonweal* (September 12, 1928).
"Concerning Old Things and New," *House Beautiful,* LXIX (January, 1931), 52.
"She's Had the Doctor!" *Atlantic Monthly,* CLI (June, 1933), 726-32. In *Reader's Digest,* XXXI (September, 1937), 91-93.
"Confidence of a Lecturer," *Commonweal,* XVIII (May 26, 1933), 100-2.
"The Dean of American Essayists," *Commonweal,* XVIII (August 18, 1933), 384-86.
"The American Father Attends His Wife's Reunion," *Scribner's* XCVI (July, 1934) 22-24.
"What Do You Expect of College for Your Daughter?" *Ladies' Home Journal,* LIII (August, 1936), 15.
"The Abundant Life in Books," *Ladies Home Journal,* LIII (September, 1936), 19.

"Are Parents Afraid of Their Children?" *Ladies' Home Journal,* LIV (March, 1937), 60.

"An Unpopular Suggestion," *Writer,* L (April, 1937), 102-3.

"Old-Time Christmases in Maine," *Ladies' Home Journal,* LIV (December, 1937), 28. In *Reader's Digest,* XXXII (January, 1938), 81-84.

"Rather Late for Christmas," *Vogue,* XCII (December 1, 1938), 87. As "Christmas Is a State of Mind," in *Reader's Digest,* XXXV (December, 1939), 39-40; in *Vogue's First Reader,* 8-12; in *Literary Cavalcade* (December, 1949).

"I Like the Younger Generation," *Ladies' Home Journal,* LVI (December, 1939), 21.

"Our Educational Heritage," *American Association of University Women Journal,* XXXIII (January, 1940), 74-79.

"Time to Oneself," *Yale Review,* XXX (September, 1940), 128-40. As "You Become Someone—Alone," in *Reader's Digest,* XXXVII (October, 1940), 37-40.

"Head and Hands Working Together," *Common Ground,* I (Autumn, 1940), 3-6.

"Progressive Education," New York *Times Magazine* (February 9, 1941), 11.

"When You Go to New England," *Harper's,* CLXXXIII (August, 1941), 294-95.

"An Ancient Democracy to a Modern," *Common Ground,* III (Winter, 1943), 65-71.

"Early Reading of the Bible," *National Parent-Teacher,* XXXIX (May, 1945), 4-6.

"Are We Afraid to Be Alone?" *Woman's Day* (October, 1949), 68.

"Sorry, We Can't Afford It," *Good Housekeeping,* CXXXI (November, 1950), 54.

"Recipe for a Magic Childhood," *Ladies' Home Journal,* LXVIII (May, 1951), 205-7.

"Must America Live in Fear?" *Coronet,* XXXIV (July, 1953), 19-23.

"A Legacy from My Childhood," *Parents Magazine,* XXVIII (August, 1953), 31.

"The Virtue of Living Fully," *House and Garden,* CIV (September, 1953), 126-27.

"What Has Happened to Common Sense?" *Coronet,* XXXVI (May, 1954), 21-25. As "What's Happened to Common Sense?" in *Reader's Digest,* LXV (July, 1954), 22-24. Also in French, Spanish, Japanese, and Portuguese editions of *Reader's Digest,* September, October, November 1954.

"The Bible in Our Kitchen," *Woman's Day* (November, 1954), p. 37.

"Courtesy on Wheels," *Atlantic Monthly*, CXCVIII (October, 1956), 78-79.
"She Misses Some Goals," *Life*, XLI (December 24, 1956), 23-25.
"Half a Dollar or 'Huckleberry Finn'?" New York *Herald-Tribune Book Review*, XXXVI (April 3, 1960), 5.
"My Novels About Maine," *Colby Library Quarterly*, VI (March, 1962), 14-20.

SECONDARY SOURCES

The biographical dictionaries and the compendia of lives of American authors contain articles on Mary Ellen Chase; their accessibility makes it unnecessary to list such materials here. Nor is it worth while to record either the numerous newspaper notices concerning Miss Chase's life and works or the brief biographical blurbs in the magazines to which she has contributed. Extensive reviews of her individual works, some of them by outstanding critics, such as Robert Hillyer, R. P. T. Coffin, Perry Miller, H. S. Commager, Sigrid Undset, may be readily located by reference to the Book Review Digest; indeed, many have already been referred to in the text.

1. *Bibliography*

CARY, RICHARD. "A Bibliography of the Published Writings of Mary Ellen Chase," *Colby Library Quarterly* (March, 1962), pp. 34-45. As complete a listing of her publications as is possible in the absence of a methodical record either by her or anyone else.

2. *Biographical and Critical*

BOYNTON, PERCY H. "Two New England Regionalists," *America in Contemporary Fiction*. Chicago, 1940. Discusses Mary Ellen Chase, along with Dorothy Canfield Fisher, as a regionalist.
DUCKETT, ELEANOR SHIPLEY. "A Portrait: 1962," *Colby Library Quarterly* (March, 1962), pp. 1-4. Glimpses of Miss Chase as she is at present, from the pen of the friend who shares her house.
IORIO, JOHN J. "Mary Ellen Chase and the Novel of Regional Crisis," *Colby Library Quarterly* (March, 1962), pp. 21-34. Miss Chase's development as a regionalist through all her novels, as well as a consideration of her style and the form of her novels.
MILBANK, HELEN KIRKPATRICK. "Mary Ellen Chase: Teacher, Writer, Lecturer," *Colby Library Quarterly* (March, 1962), pp. 5-13. Valuable as an estimate of Miss Chase as a teacher and lecturer.
TAVES, ISABELLA. *Successful Women*. New York: Books Inc., 1943. Journalistic reporting on Miss Chase's life and work as writer and teacher.

Index

All works by Mary Ellen Chase are followed by (MEC); *names of characters from these works are followed by the title—in parentheses—of the work in which they appear.*